Printed in China
孔子学院总部赠送
Donated by Confucius Institute Headquarters

国家出版基金项目
NATIONAL PUBLICATION FOUNDATION

CHINESE RED
中国红

传统乐器

Traditional Chinese Musical Instruments

肖迪◎编著

全国百佳图书出版单位
APETIME
时代出版 时代出版传媒股份有限公司
黄山书社

图书在版编目(CIP)数据

传统乐器：汉英对照 / 肖迪编著. ——合肥：黄山书社, 2012.2

（中国红）

ISBN 978-7-5461-2644-9

Ⅰ. ①传… Ⅱ. ①肖… Ⅲ. ①民族乐器—中国—汉、英 Ⅳ. ①J632

中国版本图书馆CIP数据核字(2012)第026416号

传统乐器

肖　迪 编著

出 版 人：任耕耘

责任编辑：朱莉莉　李　南　　　　　　　特约编辑：朱昌爱

责任印制：戚　帅　李　磊　　　　　　　装帧设计：商子庄

出版发行：时代出版传媒股份有限公司（http://www.press-mart.com）
　　　　　黄山书社（http://www.hsbook.cn）
　　　　　（合肥市蜀山区翡翠路1118号出版传媒广场7层　邮编：230071）

经　　销：新华书店　　　　　　　　　　营销电话：0551-3533762　3533768

印　　刷：合肥精艺印刷有限公司　　　　电　话：0551-4859368

开　　本：710×875　1/16　　　　印张：11.5　　　　字数：147千字

版　　次：2012年4月第1版　　2012年4月第1次印刷

书　　号：ISBN 978-7-5461-2644-9　　　　定价：59.00元

中国传统的音乐文化源远流长，作为不同时代音乐文化的标志，中国乐器的种类更是异彩纷呈：悠扬的箫笛，古雅的琴筝，热烈的锣鼓，嘹亮的唢呐……不同材质、不同音色的乐器，体现出不同时代和民族的审美情趣，展示了中国人的智慧和创造力，演绎着中国传统文化特有的气质。

There is a long history of traditional musical culture in China. Serving as the symbol of the musical culture in each historical period, Chinese musical instruments offer colorful varieties: from the melodious vertical flute (*Xiao*) and flute (*Di*), through the quaint and elegant 7-stringed zither (*Qin*) and 25-stringed zither (*Zheng*), to the exciting gong and drums, resonant *Suo Na* trumpet (a woodwind instrument) and more. The array of Chinese musical instruments derived from different materials with various tones and sounds has reflected the aesthetic tastes endeared in different time periods as well as by different ethnic groups. They have demonstrated the wisdom and creativity of Chinese people, interpreting the unique qualities encompassed in traditional Chinese culture.

By collecting a large number of texts and

本书在收集大量图文资料的基础上，讲述了中国传统乐器的产生与发展，分门别类地展示了传统乐器的外形、结构与音乐特性，并且穿插了许多关于乐器的有趣传说，希望读者通过本书能够了解中国乐器，体悟中国传统音乐的哲思与意境，感受中国各民族的风土人情。

graphics, this book introduces the origin and development of Chinese traditional musical instruments, describes the categorized shapes, structures and musical features of traditional musical instrument, and intersperses many interesting legends about these musical instruments. We hope that through this book, readers can understand Chinese musical instruments, realize the philosophical ideas and artistic conception embodied in Chinese traditional music, and experience various ethnic traditions throughout China.

目 录 Contents

穿越千年的乐音
Melody Through Thousands of Years

中国乐器有着悠久、深厚的历史传统，古人留下了众多极富特色的民族器乐，这些器乐除了在传统歌舞中的演奏外，在民间的婚丧喜庆、风俗节日等活动中也发挥着极其重要的作用。追溯中国乐器的发展历程，仿佛能听到袅袅乐音穿越千年而来。

Chinese musical instruments have enjoyed a time-honored and profound history and tradition. Chinese ancestors have left a multitude of highly distinctive ethnic musical instruments which are not only performed on traditional dance and music occasions, but also play a significant part in such events as weddings, funerals, celebrations, birthday parties, folk activities and festivals. Tracking the development process of Chinese musical instruments, we seem to hear the melody drawing from thousands of years ago.

> 最早的乐器

在数千年的文明历程中，中华民族创造了辉煌灿烂的音乐文化。而作为音乐的物质载体，中国古代乐器的产生年代比史籍的记载要早得多。1987年，在河南省舞阳县城北的贾湖新石器时代遗址中，出土了一批猛禽腿骨制成的骨笛。骨笛长约20多厘米，上面开有小孔，形制规范，至今仍可吹奏出旋律。这些距今约8000年的骨笛，不仅是中

> The Earliest Musical Instruments

In its civilization process over several thousands of years, Chinese people have created a splendid culture of music. As physical carriers of music, ancient Chinese musical instruments have much earlier records than historical books. In 1987, a number of flutes made out of the leg bones of raptors were unearthed among other relics from the *Jiahu* Neolithic era ruins in the north part of Wuyang County, Henan Province of

• 贾湖骨笛（新石器时代）
Jiahu Bone Flute (Neolithic Period)

国目前发现最早的乐器，也是世界上迄今为止发现年代较早、制作水平较高的吹奏乐器。它表明中国人的祖先在全世界率先进入了原始音乐的文明时期。除了骨笛之外，产生于新石器时代的远古乐器还有浙江省河姆渡文化遗址出土的骨哨、仰韶文化遗址西安半坡村出土的埙等。这些古乐器向人们展示了中华民族的智慧和创造力。

China. The bone flute, which is 20-odd centimeter long and with small openings on the surface of its regularly shaped body, can still play a melody today. These 8,000 year-old bone flutes are not only the earliest musical instruments found in China, but also the quite primitive wind instruments with the highest manufacturing level existing in the world. They indicate Chinese ancestors were the first in the world to enter the civilization period of primitive music. In addition to the bone flutes, other ancient musical instruments from the Neolithic era include bone whistles discovered in the *Hemudu* Cultural ruins in Zhejiang Province, an ancient ocarina (*Xun*) from the *Yangshao* Cultural ruins unearthed in Banpo village in Xi'an, Shaanxi Province and others. All these ancient musical instruments have demonstrated to world the wisdom and creativity of Chinese people.

- **长葛骨哨（新石器时代）**

  在河南长葛县石固遗址的裴李岗文化墓葬里，发现两件用禽类肢骨制成的骨哨。哨长约七八厘米，有一个椭圆形扁孔。经研究人员实验，堵住两端，吹气入孔可发出音响。最初的骨哨也许是诱捕野兽的狩猎工具。

  Changge Bone Whistle (Neolithic Period)

  Among the findings unearthed from the *Peiligang* cultural tombs in *Shigu* ruins, located in Changge County, Henan Province, there are two bone whistles made of the bones of bird's limbs. They are around 7 to 8 centimeters long with a flat hole in oval shape. According to the researchers' experiment, with the whistle's both ends blocked, it can deliver sounds when air is blown into the opening. The earliest bone whistle might be a hunting tool used to attract the animals.

> 礼乐之器——先秦时期

商周时期，随着生产力的发展，各种乐器层出不穷，但乐器的实际功能远远不止于娱乐或欣赏。作为礼乐制度的重要组成部分，乐器是权力的象征。在各种祭祀和宫宴等活动中，乐器被用来炫耀统治者和贵族的地位。

西周时期，有记载的乐器约有七十种之多，按照制作材质可分为金、石、土、革、丝、木、匏、竹八类，称为"八音"。在这七十多种乐器中，一般以钟、磬等打击乐器为主，弦乐器和管乐器也包含其中。当举行隆重的祭祀仪式和盛大的宴会时，乐队所用乐器的规模十分壮观。在祭天、祭地、祭祖三种仪式中，乐队所配备的钟磬及其他乐器的种类、形制、规格都有不同

> Ritual Musical Instruments: the Period before Qin Dynasty

In the Shang Dynasty (1600 B.C.-1046 B.C.) and Zhou Dynasty (1046 B.C.-256 B.C.), as productivity progressed, various musical instruments came out one after another. However, the practical functions of musical instruments were far more than mere entertainment or appreciation. As an important constituent portion of the ritualistic and musical system, the musical instrument was a symbol of power. In various events of worship, rituals and palace feasts, musical instruments were used to show off the status of the rulers and aristocrats.

In the Western Zhou Dynasty (1046 B.C.-771 B.C.), there were over 70 musical instruments recorded and classified, according to the manufacture materials, into eight categories called

的规定。西周宫廷设有专人从事乐器的制作、保管与维修，足见当时宫廷乐队的规模之庞大。

　　春秋战国时期，在诸侯国之间的外交活动中，乐器常常作为相互馈赠的礼物。有的时候，诸侯王公还会将乐器连同演奏的乐工一起赐给贵族享用。作为中国乐器发展的一个重要的阶段，这一时期乐器的种类之多、制作之精、性能之完备，可以说是发生了质的飞跃。最能够集中反映春秋战国时期乐器成

"eight sounds" (*Ba Yin*): metal, stone, clay, leather, silk, wood, gourd, and bamboo. Among the 70-plus instruments, the primary tools were the percussion instruments such as bells and musical stone (*Qing*), while string and wind instruments were also included. When solemn rituals and grand feasts were held, the lineup of the instruments used by the band was spectacular. In the three rituals of worshiping heaven, earth and ancestors, the types, shapes and specifications of the bells, musical stone or other musical instruments equipped by the band were all prescribed differently. The Western Zhou imperial court had specialists assigned to take charge of the

• "回"纹铜铙（商）
铜铙是一种古老的打击乐器，外形酷似合起来的两片瓦，使用时凹形口朝上，用木槌敲击，声音雄浑空阔，悠扬辽远。

Bronze Cymbal with Fretwork (Shang Dynasty, 1600 B.C.-1046 B.C.)

Bronze cymbal is a very old percussion instrument. It looks like two tiles conjoint together. When it is played, the concave side is facing upward and beaten with a wood hammer. It gives muscular and expansive sounds with far-reaching effects.

● 青铜甬钟（西周）

甬钟是西周时期的青铜打击乐器，由铜铙发展而来，因最上面的平面之上立有"甬柱"而得名。

Bronze Column Bell (Western Zhou Dynasty, 1046 B.C.-771 B.C.)

Column bell was a percussion instrument made of bronze in the Western Zhou Dynasty. It evolved from bronze cymbal. It is named from the "column" standing on its top surface.

manufacture, storage and maintenance of the musical instruments, which shows the great scale of the musical instruments that the court owned at that time.

In the Spring and Autumn and Warring States Period (770 B.C.-221 B.C.), musical instrument were often used as presents in diplomatic activities between the vassal states. Sometimes, the lord of a vassal state would bestow the instrument together with the musician on the noblemen for their enjoyment. This period was a significant phase of Chinese musical instrument development, a qualitative leap of the instrument was evidenced in its great variety, delicacy of the handicraft as well as the completion in the musical performance. The most typical musical instruments in the Spring and Autumn and Warring States Period were indisputably the massive number of instruments excavated from the Tomb of Marquis Yi of Zeng. This tomb dating back to early Warring States Period was discovered in *Leigudun* in Sui County, Hubei Province in 1978. There are totally 125 pieces of musical instruments in 9 categories unearthed from the tomb, which constituted the bell and musical stone band used by the tomb owner to banquet honored guests before his death. Some of the instruments unearthed were

就的，首推曾侯乙墓出土的大量乐器。曾侯乙墓是1978年在湖北省随县擂鼓墩发现的战国早期墓葬，墓中出土的乐器共有九种一百二十五件，由其组成的地下乐队是墓主人生前宴饮礼宾所用的钟磬乐队。其中的一些乐器制作具有很高的科技水准。曾侯乙墓乐器中成套编钟的出土，是中国音乐文化史、科技史、乃至世界文明史的重大发现，甚至被一些国际学者称为"世界第八大奇迹"。

manufactured at a very high technology level. The whole set of the serials bells (*Bian Zhong*) unearthed from the Tomb of Marquis Yi of Zeng is a significant discovery in the history of Chinese music, science and technology, and even in the history of world civilization. The discovery was even dubbed by some international scholars as the "8th wonder of the world".

● 青铜錞于（战国）
錞于是与鼓相配合的古代军乐器，圆筒形，上大而下小，下部中空，顶上有纽，演奏时用绳悬挂起来，用槌敲击发声。
Bronze *Chun Yu* (Warring States Period, 475 B.C.-221 B.C.)
Chun Yu was an ancient military musical instrument used in combination with drums. Cast in the shape of a tube with a broad top and a narrow bottom, the *Chun Yu* is hollow in its lower part, and has a knob set on the top to hang it up with a rope so as to be knocked by a hammer for sounds.

古代乐器的八音分类法

八音分类法是中国历史上最早的乐器科学分类法，出现于西周时期。人们将当时的乐器按制作材料分为金、石、土、革、丝、木、匏、竹八类。后来，"八音"也泛指乐器。

"金"指金属乐器，大多由铜或铜锡混合制成。古代的金属乐器，虽种类繁多，但其中最主要的是钟类乐器。钹、锣等也是金属乐器，它们的共同特性是声音洪亮、音质清脆、音色柔和。

"石"指石制乐器，主要指以坚硬的大理石或玉石制成的石磬，石质越坚硬，声音就越铿锵洪亮。

"土"指的是泥土制成的陶类乐器，主要包括埙和缶。埙的历史悠久，是吹奏乐器；缶的形状很像一个小缸或火钵，属于打击乐器。

"革"是指以野兽皮革制成的乐器，最主要的是鼓。鼓也是古人最初使用的乐器之一。

"丝"指的是用蚕丝制弦，再做成的乐器。在商周以前，丝弦乐器只有琴和瑟两种；秦汉以后才出现了筝、箜篌、阮咸、秦琴、三弦、琵琶、胡琴等。这类乐器在中国传统乐器里最富于代表性。

"木"是指木制乐器，最初有柷、敔、拍板等，后来有木鱼、梆子等，都属于打击乐器。

"匏"原指葫芦，古称"匏瓜"，古人用干老的匏瓜制成乐器，就是匏类乐器。匏类乐器包括笙和竽等簧片乐器。

"竹"是指竹类制成的乐器，主要有箫、笛和管，都属于吹管乐器。

Eight-sound Classification of Ancient Musical Instruments

Debuting in the Western Zhou Dynasty (1046 B.C.-771 B.C.), the eight-sound classification was the earliest scientific classification of musical instruments in China's history. People at that time divided the musical instruments, according to the materials they were made of, into eight different classifications, namely metal, stone, silk, bamboo, gourd, clay, leather, and wood. Later, the term "eight sounds" was used as a synonym for all musical instruments.

"Metal" refers to instruments made of metal - mostly a mixture of copper and tin. Although there was a great variety of metal musical instruments in ancient times, bells were predominant among them all. Cymbals and gongs were also made of metal. They shared the feature of sonorous and ringing sound with a crisp but soft tone, which is representative enough for the metal sounds of Chinese musical instruments.

"Stone" means the instrument made of stone. It usually refers to the musical stone (*Qing*) which is made of solid marble or jade. The harder the stone is, the more resounding effects could it produce.

"Clay" means the ceramic instruments made of clay, such as ocarina (*Xun*) and clay pot (*Fou*). Ocarina is a wind instrument with a very long history and clay pot is a percussion instrument which looks like a small jar or fire pot.

"Leather" refers to an instrument made of animal skin - mainly drums. The drum is one of the first musical instruments used by ancient people.

"Silk" refers to the instruments with their strings made of natural silk. Prior to the Shang Dynasty (1600 B.C.-1046 B.C.) and Zhou Dynasty (1046 B.C.-256 B.C.), there were only two stringed instruments, 7-stringed zither (*Qin*) and 50-stringed zither with moveable bridges (*Se*). After the Qin Dynasty (221 B.C.-206 B.C.) and the Han Dynasty (206 B.C.- 220 A.D.), more stringed instruments began to appear, such as 25-stringed zither (*Zheng*), Chinese harp (*Kong Hou*), moon-shaped lute (*Ruan Xian*), flower-shaped lute (*Qin Qin*), three strings (*San Xian*), pear-shaped lute (*Pi Pa*) and fiddle (*Hu Qin*). These are the most representative tools in Chinese traditional musical instruments.

"Wood" refers to the instruments made of wood. They were percussion instruments such as the wooden box (*Zhu*), tiger-shaped instrument (*Yu*) and clapper (*Pai Ban*) among others in the beginning. Later, instruments such as wooden knocker (*Mu Yu*) and wooden stick (*Bang Zi*) appeared.

"Gourd" was originally for gourds, also known as *Pao Gua* in ancient times. When people used old and dried-out gourds to make musical instruments, such instruments are gourd instruments. This category includes reed instruments such as *Sheng* (free reed mouth organ with finger holds) and *Yu* (free reed mouth large organ with finger holes).

"Bamboo" mainly refers to wind instruments made of bamboo, such as vertical flute, flute and oboe.

彩绘陶坐部伎乐女俑（隋）

Painted Ceramic Figurine of a Sitting Female Musician (Sui Dynasty, 581-618)

> 包容与创新——秦汉到
隋唐

　　秦汉时期，宫廷中设立了专门的音乐机构"乐府"，其主要职能是制乐和为宫廷活动服务。乐府的设立有力地推动了音乐和乐器的发展。汉代流行的相和歌、鼓吹乐、郊祀乐歌、歌舞百戏等各类音乐，都在乐府音乐活动中得到了提高与发展。而相和歌中常用的笙、笛、琴、

> Tolerance and Innovation: From the Qin and Han Dynasties to the Sui and Tang Dynasties

In the Qin Dynasty (221 B.C.-206 B.C.) and the Han Dynasty (206 B.C.-220 A.D.), the imperial court set up a special music organization called *Yue Fu*, whose major function was to compose music and serve the court activities. The establishment of music organization forcefully pushed forward the development of music and musical instruments. Various popular music in the Han Dynasty, including *Xiang He* songs, wind and percussion music, suburban ritual music and songs, musical dance and acrobatics music, were all promoted and developed in the musical events held

• 抚琴俑（汉）
Figurine of a 7-stringed Zither Player (Han Dynasty, 206 B.C.- 220 A.D.)

• 饮宴奏乐画像砖（东汉）
Brick Painting of Musical Banquet (Eastern Han Dynasty, 25-220)

瑟、筝等丝竹乐器，以及鼓吹乐常用的鼓、箫、角等管乐器和打击乐器也得到了极大的发展。后来随着西汉时期张骞出使西域，使西域与中原的音乐文化得以交流，西域少数民族的乐器开始传入中原，受到汉族的喜爱。

魏晋时期，随着社会的分裂动荡和各民族的迁徙融合，经由丝绸之路从西域传入的乐器，如琵琶、阮咸、羌笛、羯鼓、箜篌等，在传统乐器中渐渐占据了明显的地位。另一方面，古琴作为一种独奏乐器，以其淡雅悠远的特点受到文人的喜爱。当时的士人阶层出现了一批不依附于宫廷的文人音乐家，如

by the music organization. Instruments made of silk and bamboo, such as *Sheng* (free reed mouth organ with finger holes), flute, 7-stringed zither, 50-stringed zither, and 25-stringed zither, often used in *Xiang He* songs, as well as wind and percussion instruments of drums, vertical flute and bugle (*Jiao*) often used in wind and percussion music, were all greatly developed. Later on, when Zhang Qian (164 B.C.-114 B.C.) traveled to the western regions as an ambassador and brought about the cultural interchange of music between the central plains of China and the western regions, the musical instruments from the ethnic minorities in the western regions began to be carried into the central plains of China and favored by the Han ethnic group.

As the turmoil of social division and the migration and mixture of ethnic groups occurred in the Wei and Jin Period (220-420), musical instruments imported from western regions by the Silk Road (a route over which Han silk fabrics and other products were transported to Southwest Asia and Europe). There were pear-shaped lute, moon-shaped lute, *Qiang* flute (a kind of flute used by Qiang ethnic group), *Jie* drum (a kind of hourglass-shaped drum used by Jie ethnic

蔡邕、嵇康、阮籍等，他们都创作了大量流传后世的琴曲，将古琴的制作与演奏技艺推向了高峰。

隋唐时期，国家统一，经济繁荣，宫廷歌舞乐"燕乐"得以发展。燕乐以琵琶为中心，同时引用

● 乐舞图黄釉扁壶（北齐）

乐舞图中五个男子均为西域胡人，中间的人正在跳"胡腾舞"，右边二人一个击掌伴唱，一个吹横笛，左边二人一人执钹，一人弹琵琶。这五个人高鼻深目，穿着胡人服饰，展现出典型的西域风情。

Yellow Glazed Jar Painted with Musical Dance (Northern Qi Dynasty, 550-577)

In the musical dance picture, the five males are from the ethnic groups in western regions. The one in the middle is dancing the *Hu Teng* dance, while the two on the right are respectively clapping hands for accompaniment and playing transverse flute. The other two on the left are respectively holding a cymbal and playing pear-shaped lute (*Pi Pa*). The five of them, featured with high noses and deeply set-in eyes, are dressed in foreign attires and display a whole different view of the western regions.

group) and Chinese harp, gradually gained conspicuous positions among the traditional instruments. On the other hand, the solo performance instrument, ancient 7-stringed zither (*Gu Qin*), drew a lot of favors from literati for its moderate and distant nature. A group of literati musicians made their appearance out of the scholarly circles, such as Cai Yong, Ji Kang and Ruan Ji, who renounced reliance on the imperial court, composed a great volume of lute music which has been passed down through generations, and pushed the craftsmanship and performance skills of ancient 7-stringed zither to the very top of the climax.

The national unification and prosperous economy in the Sui Dynasty (581-618) and Tang Dynasty (618-907) paved the way for the development of court dance music *Yan* music. Centered on pear-shaped lute (*Pi Pa*), *Yan* music made use of a lot of new instruments imported from the frontier regions and foreign countries, such as pear-shaped lute, Chinese harp, double reed oboe (*Bi Li*), flute, *Sheng* (free reed mouth organ with finger holes) and *Jie* drum. Their performance levels reached a historic climax in the Tang Dynasty. Compared with the Wei Dynasty, Jin Dynasty

- 敦煌壁画《反弹琵琶图》（唐）

Mural of Dunhuang *Playing Pear-shaped Lute (Pi Pa) in the Reverse Way* (Tang Dynasty, 618-907)

诸多从边疆和国外传入的新乐器，如琵琶、箜篌、筚篥、笛、笙、羯鼓等，演奏的水平在唐代均达到历史的高峰。与魏晋南北朝相比，唐代鼓类乐器的使用增多，在拉弦乐器的发展上也有了新的突破，如奚琴、轧筝的出现，开辟了乐器演奏的一个新的领域。

and Southern and Northern Dynasties, the Tang Dynasty witnessed more use of drum instruments and experienced new breakthroughs in the development of the bowed string instruments, such as *Xi* fiddle and *Ya* bowed-zither, the appearance of which ushered in a new area in musical instrument performances.

五声音阶

五声音阶是中国古代音乐的调式基础，"五声"指"宫、商、角、徵、羽"，相当于现代音乐的C、D、E、G、A五个音阶。其特点在于没有半音阶（小二度）音程，所以又称为"全音五声音阶"。五声音阶中的每一个音都可以当主音以建立调式，所以可形成五种不同的调式。先秦著作《管子·地员篇》中，正式记载了计算五声音阶中各音的弦长比例的数学方法，史称"三分损益法"，并完整记述了"宫、商、角、徵、羽"的名称。

The Pentatonic Scale

The pentatonic (five-sound) scale was the mode basis of ancient Chinese music. The five scales are marked as *Gong, Shang, Jue, Zhi,* and *Yu,* in equivalence to the scales of C, D, E, G and A in modern music. Its feature lies in the lack of chromatic (minor second) intervals; hence it is also called the "whole-tone pentatonic scale". In this five-sound scale, each sound can act as the key note to build up the mode; therefore, there are five different modes. In the period before Qin Dynasty (221 B.C.-206 B.C.), the *Round Earth* Chapter of *Guan Zi* formally recorded the mathematic method, historically known as *San Fen Sun Yi Fa* (the method of one-third addition or detraction), to calculate the proportional cord length of each of the five sounds, and also had a full description for the names of the five sounds.

> 民间乐器的崛起——宋元明清

宋元时期，戏曲和曲艺得到不断地发展，作为伴奏的戏乐乐器也随之发展和提高。戏乐乐器以笛、鼓和板组成的乐队形式出现，编制非常丰富。一些为戏曲伴奏的器乐曲还可以独立演出。宋元时期独立的器乐演奏，以宫廷教坊乐的器乐最为典型。主要乐器有属于气鸣乐

> The Rise of the Folk Instrument: Song, Yuan, Ming, and Qing Dynasties

In the Song Dynasty (960-1279) and Yuan Dynasty (1206-1368), as opera and vocal art progressed, musical instruments which accompanied opera music were advanced and improved accordingly. The opera band appeared in rich formation, composed of such instruments as flute, drums and clappers. Some of these musical instruments would perform solos. In the Song Dynasty and Yuan Dynasty, the solo performances were typically those played in the teaching school music (*Jiao Fang* music) of the royal court. The major instruments

● 定窑八角镂雕兽首响铃器（宋）
8-cornered Sounding Instrument with Piercing-sculptured Animal Head from the *Ding* Kiln (Song Dynasty, 960-1279)

器的竽篪、笙、排箫、埙；属于弦乐器的琵琶、箜篌、筝、嵇琴；属于打击乐器的拍板、钹、杖鼓、大鼓、羯鼓、鼗鼓等。在乐队中，弓弦乐器逐渐开始取代琵琶，占据重要地位，尤其是奚琴、马尾胡琴的发展，在中国乐器史上有特殊的意义。

● 吹笛子伎乐木雕塑像（元）
Wooden Sculpture of a Musician Playing Flute (Yuan Dynasty, 1206-1368)

played included the aerophones of double reed oboe, *Sheng* (free reed mouth organ with finger holes), panpipes and ocarina; the string instruments of pear-shaped lute (*Pi Pa*), Chinese harp, 25-stringed zither and *Ji* zither (a kind of zither which is said to be invented by Ji Kang, a Chinese famous literati); and percussion instruments of clapper, cymbal, Korean Tambourin (a long drum used by the Korean ethnic group), bass drum, *Jie* drum and pellet drum. In the band, bowed string instruments began to replace the pear-shaped lute and take on important roles. Among them, the development of *Xi* fiddle, horsetail fiddle and others assumed special significance in the history of Chinese musical instruments.

In the Ming Dynasty (1368-1644) and Qing Dynasty (1644-1911), Chinese musical instruments and the art of musical instruments reached the summit of prosperity. In terms of solo-performed instruments, ancient 7-stringed zither was still the key instrument in the circle of literati music. Many literati not only advocated the study of zither, but also compiled the zither melodies handed down from ancient times into composition collections. There were also different schools of ancient 7-stringed

一宿因缘邃中媒词聊以 懴泥陌雷時我作陶歌音 何必尊前面發红唐寅

● 唐寅《陶谷赠词卷轴》（明）

图中文士拈须倚坐榻上，旁置笔墨纸砚，歌女束发高髻，坐弹琵琶，情态生动逼真。

Scroll of Offering Poetry at Taogu by Tang Yin (Ming Dynasty, 1368-1644)

A vivid and picturesque scene with the man of letters sitting on the bed stroking his beard, the writing brush, ink stick, paper and inkstone ready by the side, while a bun-haired female singer sitting and playing pear-shaped lute.

明清时期，中国的乐器与器乐艺术达到了繁荣的顶峰。在独奏乐方面，古琴乐仍然是文人音乐的重要乐种。不少文人提倡琴学，经常将古代传承下来的琴曲编纂成谱集。古琴的演奏还形成了各种不同的流派。同时，琵琶艺术也获得了很大的发展，不仅涌现了许多琵琶演奏名家，而且也在各地产生了众多的演奏流派。在乐器的合奏方面，流行于北方民间、风格热烈欢快的鼓吹乐，与流行于江南等地、风格优雅华丽的丝竹乐交相辉映。

zither performance. Meanwhile, the art of pear-shaped lute also received great development. Not only did a great deal of famed pear-shaped lute performers emerge, but a multitude of different schools of performances in various places also came into being. As for the ensemble of musical instruments, the cheerful, fast-paced style of wind and percussion music, which was prevalent in the local society in the north, and the splendid, elegant silk and bamboo music in the regions south of the Yangtze River added radiance and beauty to each other.

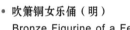

• 吹箫铜女乐俑（明）
Bronze Figurine of a Female Musician Playing Vertical Flute (Ming Dynasty, 1368-1644)

中国乐器大家族

The Extended Family of Chinese Musical Instruments

经过几千年的发展，中国传统乐器已有上千种之多。按照演奏方式的不同，一般可分为吹奏乐器、拉弦乐器、弹拨乐器和打击乐器四大类。

Through thousands of years of development, the total number of traditional Chinese musical instruments has grown to more than 1,000 kinds. According to the ways they are played, these instruments are generally classified into four categories: the wind instrument, the bowed string instrument, the plucked string instrument and the percussion instrument.

> 吹奏乐器

吹奏乐器的发音体大多为竹制或木制。根据其起振方法不同，可分为三类：一类以气流吹入吹口激起管柱振动，如箫、笛、口笛等；一类是气流通过哨片吹入，使管柱振动，如唢呐、海笛、管子等；还有一类是气流通过簧片引起管柱振动，如笙、排笙、巴乌等。

> Wind Instrument

The sounding body of the wind instrument is mostly made of bamboo or wood. Based on the way the vibration is generated, there are three different types: the first type are instruments like vertical flute (*Xiao*), flute (*Di*) and small transverse bamboo flute (*Kou Di*) , whose vibration is generated by blowing air directly into the opening to make the pipe vibrate; the second type are instruments like *Suo Na* trumpet (a woodwind instrument), *Hai Di* (small *Suo Na* trumpet) and *Guan Zi* (cylindrical double reed wind instrument), which incorporate a mouthpiece to force the inflow of air to vibrate the tube; the last type are instruments like *Sheng* (free

• 浙江余姚河姆渡出土的陶埙（河姆渡文化）
Ceramic Ocarina Unearthed from the *Hemudu* Cultural Ruins in Yuyao County, Zhejiang Province (*Hemudu* Culture)

埙

埙是中国最古老的吹奏乐器之一，大约有7000年的历史。埙上端有吹口，底部呈平面，侧壁开有音孔。

相传埙起源于狩猎工具。古时候，人们常常用绳子系上一个石球或者泥球，投出去击打鸟兽。有的球体中间是空的，抢起来能发出声音。后来人们觉得挺好玩，就拿来吹，于是这种空心泥球就慢慢演变成了埙。也有人认为最初可能是先民们模仿鸟兽叫声而制作了埙，用以诱捕猎物。

埙最初大多是用石头或骨头制作的，后来发展成为陶制，形状也有多种，如扁圆形、椭圆形、球形、鱼形和梨形等。最早的埙只有一个音孔，后来逐渐发展为多孔，一直到公元前3世纪末期才出现六音孔埙。浙江省余

reed mouth organ with finger holds), Pai *Sheng* and *Ba Wu* (side-blown free reed pipe with finger holes), in which the air flows through a reed into the vibrating tube.

Ocarina

The approximately 7,000-year-old ocarina (*Xun*) is one of the oldest Chinese wind instruments, with a blowing hole on top, flat bottom, and sound holes on the side wall.

Tradition has it that ocarina originally came from a hunting tool. In ancient times, people used to tie a stone ball or clay ball at one end of a rope, which was flung at a target of birds or animals. Some of the balls were hollow so that on rapid retrieving, they might catch the wind and give a sound. People later took the ball to play for fun, and by and by, the hollow clay ball evolved

• 五音孔陶埙（商）
Five-sound-hole Ceramic Ocarina (Shang Dynasty, 1600 B.C.-1046 B.C.)

• 马面形童玩小瓷埙（宋）
Small Children's Toy of Ocarina with a
Horse Face (Song Dynasty, 960-1279)

姚县河姆渡遗址出土的陶埙，呈椭圆形，只有吹孔而无音孔，距今约7000年。陕西西安半坡村仰韶文化遗址出土的陶哨，形似橄榄，只有一个吹孔，用细泥捏塑而成，是埙的原始形态之一，距今约6000年。

商代的埙比原始时期和夏代有了较大的发展，形体多为平底卵形。战国时期陶埙也为平底卵形，但也有其他形状的。秦汉以后，埙主要用于宫廷音乐。在宫廷音乐

into ocarina. Some people also believed ocarina was created to mimic the sound of birds and animals for the purpose of attracting and capturing prey.

Originally, ocarina was mostly made of stones and bones. It later developed into ceramic ware in various shapes, such as the oblate, oval, ball, fish, and pear shapes. The earliest ocarina had only one sound hole. Multiple holes were later developed. The six-hole ocarina didn't appear until the end of the 3rd century B.C. The ceramic oval ocarina, which was unearthed from the *Hemudu* cultural ruins in Yuyao county, Zhejiang Province, only has a blowing hole with no sound hole and can be dated back to around 7,000 years ago. The ceramic whistle discovered in the *Yangshao* cultural ruins at Banpo village in Xi'an, Shaanxi Province, takes the similar shape of an olive with only one blowing hole. Kneaded with fine silt, the whistle was one of the primitive forms of ocarina and can be traced back to about 6,000 years ago.

In comparison with the early primitive period and the Xia Dynasty (the 21st Century B.C.-the 16th Century B.C.), the Shang Dynasty (1600 B.C.-1046 B.C.) had seen a great development in

中，埙分成颂埙和雅埙两种。颂埙形体较小，像个鸡蛋，音响稍高；雅埙形体较大，音响浑厚低沉，常常和一种竹子做的吹管乐器"篪"配合演奏。在中国最早的诗歌总集《诗经》里就有"伯氏吹埙，仲氏吹篪"的诗句，意思是说兄弟两人，一个吹埙一个吹篪，表达和睦亲善的手足之情。

ocarina, mostly in the shape of an egg with flat bottom. In the Warring States Period (475 B.C.-221 B.C.), the ceramic ocarina also appeared in other shapes than the common egg shape with a flat bottom. After the Qin Dynasty (221 B.C.-206 B.C.) and Han Dynasty (206 B.C.- 220 A.D.), ocarina was mostly used in court music and was divided into two kinds: *Song* ocarina and *Ya* ocarina. *Song* ocarina was smaller, like a chicken egg with high pitch; *Ya* ocarina was bigger, with a deep, low, and vigorous sound, and was always accompanied by *Chi*, a wind instrument made of bamboo. In the earliest anthology of Chinese poetry, *The Classic of Poetry*, there's a line which reads, "Bo blows ocarina, and Zhong blows *Chi*", which depicts two brothers, one playing ocarina while the other playing *Chi*, in a close and loving relationship with each other.

● **红油金漆龙埙（清）**
此埙通体髹红色桐油，周身饰描金色二龙戏珠纹和祥云纹，纹饰以黑漆勾勒，形象生动，色彩艳丽，充分显示出清宫皇家御用乐器富丽堂皇的特点。据清代文献记载，红油金漆龙埙一般用在各种坛庙祭祀与殿陛朝会时的中和韶乐之中。

Ocarina with Dragons Painted in Red and Golden Colors (Qing Dynasty, 1644-1911)
The body of the ocarina is painted in red oil paint with golden-line traced figures of two dragons vying for a ball as well as patterns of auspicious clouds. The lively patterns outlined by black paints and bright colors have fully demonstrated the splendid features of the imperial musical instrument in the court of Qing Dynasty. According to the literature in Qing Dynasty, the ocarina with dragons painted in red and golden colors was usually used in the *Zhong He Shao Yue* (a kind of imperial music used in fetes, court assemblies and banquets) in various rituals and worships or the court assemblies.

笛

笛，又称"竹笛"、"笛子"、"横笛"等，古时称为"横吹"，是中国最具特色的吹奏乐器之一，它的历史可以上溯到新石器时代的骨笛，距今已有8000余年。骨笛是人类先民在狩猎时用来诱捕猎物的一种工具，用鸟禽的肢骨加工而成。后来，人们开始用竹料制笛。笛在汉代以前多为竖吹，后逐渐变为横吹，与竖吹的箫等乐器区分开来。

竹笛流传地域很广，种类繁多，而使用最普遍是梆笛和曲笛。

梆笛因多用于北方梆子戏的伴

● 吹笛乐伎玉带板（唐）
Jade Belt Board with Musician Playing Flute (Tang Dynasty, 618-907)

Flute

Flute (*Di*), also known as bamboo flute, *Di Zi* and transverse flute, were called *Heng Chui* in ancient times. As one of the most special wind instruments in China, the history of flute can be traced back to the bone flute in the Neolithic era around 8,000 years ago. Bone flute was a hunting tool wrought out of the limb bones of birds and used by ancient people to attract and capture preys. People later turned to bamboo as the material for flute. Flute was blown vertically before the Han Dynasty (206 B.C.-220 A.D.), but was gradually changed into a transverse instrument and differentiated from the vertically played vertical flute (*Xiao*).

Bamboo flute has prevailed in many areas and has appeared in a great variety of forms, the most popular of which are *Bang* flute and *Qu* flute.

Bang flute acquired its name from its accompaniment in the music of *Bang Zi* opera in northern China. It's slim and short, with a bright and powerful, high-pitched tone, and has a highlighted emphasis on the tongue skills while playing it. *Bang* flute boasts the expression of vigorously bold and unconstrained interest, as well as lively

膜孔，笛身左端第二个孔，用来贴笛膜。笛膜一般用芦苇膜做成，经揉纹后取一小方块使用。经过气流振动笛膜，笛子便能发出清脆明亮的声音。

Diaphragm hole is the second hole from the left, covered with flute diaphragm, made of the membrane of the reed after being kneaded and wrought. After the air is blown in, it goes through and vibrates the flute diaphragm, a crisp and bright sound will thus be produced.

吹孔，笛身左端第一个孔。演奏者通过吹孔把气灌进笛管内，使笛膜和竹管内的竹簧产生振动。

Blowing hole is the first hole from the left side of the flute. The performer blows air into the tube of the flute so as to vibrate the flute diaphragm (*Di Mo*) as well as the reed inside the bamboo.

音孔，按指孔，共有六个，分别开闭这些音孔，就能发出高低不同的音。

Sound holes are the holes on which fingers press. There are six of them. Opening or covering these sound holes will produce sounds of high or low tones.

助音孔，可用来调高音，以美化音色、增大音量，也可以用来系飘穗。

Assistant sound holes are two in number, They are used to adjust the treble so as to beautify the tone and enhance the volume. Sometimes, a string of tassel is tied here for decoration.

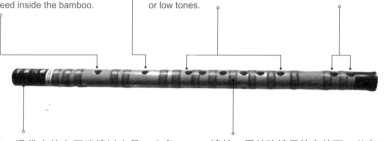

镶口，通常在笛身两端镶以牛骨、牛角、玉石或象牙，作为保护和装饰。

Xiang Kou is the openings on both ends where cow bone, bull horn, jade or ivory adornments are placed for protection or decoration purpose.

缠丝，用丝弦缠于笛身外面，共有二十一至二十四道，起保护笛身避免破裂的作用。

Chan Si is the silk string coiling around the body of flute in 21 to 24 rounds to protect the body from cracking.

- 竹笛

笛身由一根竹管做成，里面去节中空成内膛。笛塞是用软木制成的塞子，装在吹孔上端管内一定的深度里。

Bamboo Flute

The body of flute is made of a bamboo pipe with unblocked chamber inside. In the pipe is inserted a plug (*Di Sai*) made of cork, at a specific length from the upper part of the blowing hole.

奏而得名。笛身细且短小，音色高亢、明亮、有力，演奏时着重于舌上技巧的运用。梆笛善于表现刚健豪放、活泼轻快的情致，具有强烈的北方色彩，这和中国北方人民所处的地域特点及生活、劳动习惯是分不开的。梆笛一般用于北方的吹歌会、评剧和梆子戏曲（如秦腔、河北梆子、蒲剧等）的伴奏，也可

and fast-paced temperament, with the typical character of the north China. It is inseparable from the geographic traits and habits in life and labor that the people in the northern China are involved in. *Bang* flute is generally performed as the accompaniment of blowing songs meeting (*Chui Ge Hui*), *Ping* opera, and *Bang Zi* opera (for example, *Qin Qiang*, Hebei *Bang Zi*, *Pu* opera, etc.). *Bang* flute can also play solo.

Qu flute is mostly used in accompanying music for operas like *Kun Qu* opera and others in the south. It is also known as *Ban* flute and *Shi* flute. Since it abounds in Suzhou City, it's also called *Su* flute. With a thick and long body, *Qu* flute produces a pure, simple and mellow sound, and requires particular breathing moves in a slim and prolonged fashion coupled with a delicate change of force exerted for the sake of the tactful, melodious tone delivered. The exquisite, and splendid music it performs endorses

• 吹笛砖雕人像（五代）
Brick Sculpture with a Flute Player (Five Dynasties, 907-960)

用来独奏。

曲笛因多用于南方昆曲等戏曲的伴奏而得名，又叫"班笛"、"市笛"等。因盛产于苏州，故又有"苏笛"之称。曲笛管身粗而长，音色淳厚、圆润，吹奏时讲究运气的绵长，力度变化细致，吹出的音色悠扬委婉，演奏的曲调优美、精致、华丽，具有浓厚的江南韵味，与北方梆笛独奏曲粗犷有力的特点形成鲜明的对照。曲笛在我国南方广为流行，适宜独奏、合奏，是昆曲等戏曲音乐、江南丝竹、苏南吹打等地方音乐中富有特色的乐器之一。

the charm of Jiangnan (south of Yangtze River), which is in stark contrast to the bold and powerful solo performance of *Bang* flute in the northern style. *Qu* flute prevails in the south of China and suits performances in both solo and ensemble. It is one of the highlighted musical instruments in such opera music as *Kun Qu* opera, as well as in local music like Jiangnan Silk and Bamboo (traditional stringed and woodwind instruments), *Su Nan Chui Da* (a wind and percussion instruments) and the like.

• **粉彩吹笛图碟（清 雍正）**
Powdered Color Plate with a Flute Player (the reign of Emperor Yongzheng during the Qing Dynasty)

柯亭笛

东汉光和年间（178—184），宦官当政，朝廷昏暗，文学家、音乐家蔡邕因对国家大事的评说得罪了宦官，被判罪充军，流放到遥远的北方。不久，朝廷大赦，蔡邕获释回家。一天，蔡邕全家到了会稽高迁（今浙江绍兴）。这里竹子成林，引起了蔡邕的逸趣，他想取竹制笛以消除旅途劳累。午后，他独自到竹林里挑竹料，可是并没有找到合适的，扫兴而归时，无意中来到一座名为"柯亭"的小巧竹亭子。他迈步进去，四边瞧瞧，忽然对着屋檐下竹子制成的柱子数了起来，数到第十六根时，突然停住了。他走上前去，对着那根柱子又看又摸，喜爱非常，喊着要把这根柱子拆下来。亭子的主人走出来说："亭子昨天才盖好，拆不得啊！你要竹子，后面竹林有

• 蔡邕像
Portrait of Cai Yong (133-192)

的是。"蔡邕着急地说："我要的竹子必须丝纹细密、又圆又直、不粗不细，你看这竹子光泽淡黄又有黑色的斑纹，从里到外都是再好不过的制笛材料。"经过反复的恳求和商议，最后蔡邕出重金请人将这第十六根竹子拆了下来，并另找竹子修好柯亭。蔡邕如获至宝，将竹子带回家中，反复把玩，爱不释手。笛子做成后，果然音色空灵通透，圆润醇厚，随着蔡邑手指翻飞，美妙的旋律或婉转、或哀怨、或激昂、或深沉，闻者无不为之陶醉动容。由于竹子取材于柯亭，乃取名"柯亭笛"。

Keting Flute

During the Guanghe Period (178-184) in the Eastern Han Dynasty (25-220), when the eunuchs held the power in degenerative court, Cai Yong, a literary writer and musicologist, offended the eunuch for his bold political comments and was consequently sentenced to being banished to an army post in exile at a faraway place in the north. A national amnesty was later announced by the court and Cai Yong was able to return home. One day, Cai Yong and his family traveled to Gaoqian in Kuaiji (today' s Shaoxing in Zhejiang Province), where the lush woods of bamboo aroused Cai Yong's interest in making a flute out of the bamboo as a pastime to dispel the exhaustion caused by the long-distance tour. After noon, he visited the bamboo woods to pick a suitable bamboo stick for the material, but he couldn't find one. As he returned in disappointment, he accidentally came to a small and compact bamboo pavilion, titled *Keting*. He strolled into the pavilion, looked around and started counting the pillars made of bamboo under the eaves. When he counted to 16, he stopped. He stepped forward, looked at the pillar and stroked it so fondly that he shouted loudly that he wanted it to be torn down. The owner of the pavilion came out and said, "The pavilion was just built yesterday. You can't tear it down. If you want the bamboo, there are plenty of them in the woods back there." Cai Yong hastily responded, "I want bamboo which is round and straight, neither thick nor slim, and with tight texture. Look at this bamboo. It has a yellowish hue and black stripes. It's utterly the best material for making a flute." After repeated begging and negotiation, Cai Yong finally offered a great sum of money and successfully got someone to tear down the sixteenth bamboo and replace them with others to restore the pavilion *Keting*. Cai Yong brought the bamboo back home like some kind of acquired treasure. He fondled it again and again, too lovingly to put it away. When the flute was made, it gave an ethereal, transparent and mellow tone, straining with Cai Yong's flying fingers for the beautiful melody of tactful rhythm in sadness, excitement, or deep mood. Anyone who heard it couldn't resist being moved and intoxicated by it. Since the bamboo was picked from *Keting*, it was called *Keting* flute.

箫

箫是一种非常古老的吹奏乐器，又名"洞箫"，与笛同源，鼻祖均为骨哨，在之后的发展中曾被称为"籥"、"篴"等。唐代以前，笛、箫通常统称为"笛"，至唐代，两者逐渐有了区别，横吹而有膜孔的称为"笛"，竖吹无膜孔的称为"箫"。箫与笛最大的区别是，箫为竖吹，管身只有音孔而没有膜孔，吹奏起来音色柔美圆润、幽远典雅。箫的演奏技巧基本上和

Vertical Flute

Vertical flute (*Xiao*), also known as *Dong Xiao*, is a very ancient wind instrument which originated from the same root as flute, namely the bone whistle, and was also called *Yue*, *Zhu*, and other names in later development. Before the Tang Dynasty (618-907), both flute and vertical flute were collectively called "flute". It was in the Tang Dynasty that they were differentiated, where flute was transverse with a mouthpiece membrane, while the vertical flute was membrane-free and vertically blown. The biggest

● 伎乐俑（唐）

Figurine of Musical Dance (Tang Dynasty, 618-907)

笛子相同，可轻松地吹奏出滑音、叠音和打音等，其灵敏度稍逊于笛，不便于演奏垛音、花舌等极有特性的技巧，而适于以恬淡、舒缓、深情的曲调表达优雅、静谧的情感。

　　箫虽然是一件简单的竹制乐器，外形朴素却内蕴贵族气质，在中国历史上的文化地位极高，为历代文人墨客所钟爱，可以媲美古琴。宋代大文豪苏东坡曾在《赤壁赋》中极写箫声之美："如怨如慕，如泣如诉，余音袅袅，不绝如缕，舞幽壑之潜蛟，泣孤舟之嫠妇。"

difference between vertical flute and flute is that vertical flute is played vertically with no membrane and only has sound holes in the body. The music vertical flute produces is gentle, mellow, far-reaching and graceful. The playing skills of vertical flute are basically the same as flute. It can freely play out glides, double tones, tapping, and so forth. However, it is not as agile and sensitive as flute, so it is not suitable for those high-demanding skills like tongue rolling, augment, and the like; nevertheless, it is capable of long-lasting, serene and lyrical tunes to express tranquil and elegant feelings.

● 唐寅《吹箫图》（明）
Vertical Flute Playing Picture by Tang Yin (Ming Dynasty, 1368-1644)

箫不仅适于独奏、重奏，还用于江南丝竹、福建南音、广东音乐、常州丝弦和河南板头乐队等民间器乐合奏以及越剧等地方戏曲的伴奏。

另外，在唐代以前的史书上所提到的"箫"，大多特指排箫。排箫由一系列管子组成，管身没有音孔，管子按由长到短的顺序排列连接在一起，底部都用塞子堵住，构成一个个独立的吹管。吹奏时，气流进入管中可产生高低不同的音调。汉唐以来的

Although vertical flute is a very simple instrument made of bamboo with a simple and plain outlook, it is intrinsically of an aristocratic quality and has not only enjoyed high cultural esteem in China's history but also has the same favorable position among poets and literati as ancient 7-stringed zither (*Gu Qin*). The literary giant of the Song Dynasty (960-1279), Su Dongpo, depicted the beautiful sound of vertical flute in his *Poem of Red Cliff* as such: "like complaint, like aspiration, like sobbing, like confiding, with the ending tone lingering around without ending, streaming like a hidden dragon through the dcpth of the valley, and sobbing like a widow abandoned in a lonely boat."

Vertical flute not only fits for solos

● 骨排箫（商末周初）
Bone Panpipes (late Shang Dynasty, 1600 B.C.-1046 B.C. and early Zhou Dynasty, 1046 B.C.-256 B.C.)

● 石排箫（春秋）
Stone Panpipes (Spring and Autumn Period, 770 B.C.-476 B.C.)

石刻、壁画以及墓俑保存了许多吹奏排箫的形象。排箫的种类繁多。从管数组成看，就有十到二十四管不等的十余种。从制作材料看，排箫除竹质外，还有骨

- 吹排箫俑（西汉）
  Figuring Playing Panpipes (Western Han Dynasty, 206 B.C.- 25A.D.)

- 吹排箫砖俑（元）
  Brick Figuring Playing Panpipes (Yuan Dynasty, 1206-1368)

and ensemble, but also applies to such local instrumental ensembles as Jiangnan Silk and Bamboo, Fujian South Tone, Guangdong music, Changzhou Silk Strings, Henan *Ban Tou* musical band and others, as well as to the accompaniment music of local operas like *Yue* opera.

In addition, the "vertical flutes" mentioned in the historical books before the Tang Dynasty (618-907) were mostly panpipes (*Pai Xiao*). Panpipes is composed of a series of pipes without sound holes, arranged from the longest to the shortest in a row. The bottom of each pipe is sealed, making each pipe an independent tube to be blown. When played, the pipes deliver different pitches as the airflow enters into the pipes. Stone carvings, murals, and tomb figurines since the Han Dynasty (206 B.C.-220 A.D.) and Tang Dynasty preserved many images of panpipes being played. There is a wide variety of different panpipes. In terms of the number of the pipes, there were more than ten different kinds of them ranging from 10 to 24 pipes. Based on the material they were made of, panpipes were also made of bones or stones in addition to bamboo. So far, the earliest bamboo panpipes known is the thirteen-pipe panpipes of Marquis

中国乐器大家族 The Extended Family of Chinese Musical Instruments

质、石质的。目前所知的最早竹质排箫实物为战国曾侯乙墓出土的曾侯乙十三管排箫，距今已有2400多年。

Yi of Zeng, unearthed from the Tomb of Marquis Yi of Zeng in the Warring States Period (475 B.C.-221 B.C.), with about 2,400 years of history.

吹箫引凤

春秋时期，秦穆公有一个名叫弄玉的女儿，长得花容月貌，而且精通音律，擅长吹笙。有天晚上，弄玉正在宫中吹笙，忽然听到隐约有乐声从远处传来，与自己的乐音相和，精妙无比。弄玉将此事告诉了父亲，恳请他寻访奏乐之人。秦穆公派去的大臣几经探寻，最后在华山找到了一位面如朗月的青年男子。此人名叫萧史，最善吹洞箫，箫声可远达数百里，令听者流连忘返。

大臣便将萧史带回朝廷。秦穆公让萧史吹起洞箫，一曲奏起，如仙乐飘飘，动听悦耳；二曲吹罢，五色祥云翩然飞至，大殿上五光十色；三曲吹毕，百鸟齐至，凤翔鹤鸣，一派仙境风光。在场众人看得目瞪口呆。弄玉见萧史不仅风度翩翩，俊朗潇洒，而且精通乐律，演奏传神，更是一见倾心。秦穆公知道女儿对此人芳心暗许，当下便把弄玉许配给了萧史。

两人成亲后，住到了穆公特地为他们起建的凤台上。两人日夜笙箫合奏，恩爱无比。这一夜，夫妇俩正在月下合奏，忽然一对金龙彩凤从空中飞来，落到凤台上。于是萧史乘龙，弄玉骑凤，双双飞升仙界，做了一对神仙眷侣。

笙箫合奏，一如琴瑟和谐，两样乐器的和鸣，成就了一段美丽姻缘。华山上有好几处景致以弄玉吹箫命名，如"玉女峰"、"引凤亭"等。

Playing Vertical Flute to Draw in the Phoenix

In the Spring and Autumn Period (770 B.C.-476 B.C.), Duke Mu of Qin State had a beloved daughter named Nong Yu, who was beautiful and well-versed in music, especially in playing *Sheng* (free reed mouth organ with finger holds). One night, when Nong Yu was playing *Sheng* in the palace, she heard some faintly played music coming from afar in perfect tune with the music she was playing. She told this to her father and asked him to locate this music player. Finally, the people sent by Duke Mu of Qin located a bright-looking young man in Hua Mountain named Xiao Shi, an expert of vertical flute, whose vertical flute music could travel sevreal hundred miles away and make the listener forget himself.

The imperial minister brought Xiao Shi back to the palace. Duke Mu of Qin requested the man to play for him. When the music started, it sounded moving and pleasant, like music floating from heaven; as the second song ended, five-colored auspicious clouds flew in and sprinkled colorful radiance over the palace hall; by the time the third song was over, hundreds of birds flocked over with a phoenix hovering and cranes calling, creating a scene of fairy dimension. All the people present were flabbergasted by the sight. Nong Yu was deeply moved by Xiao Shi's gentle and handsome appearance, as well as his expertise in music and phenomenal performance. Having felt his daughter's crush on this gentleman, Duke Mu married her to him on the spot.

After they married, the couple moved to the Phoenix Platform, which Duke Mu built for them. Day in and day out, the couple would tune their *Sheng* and vertical flute into a harmonious ensemble. One night, the couple was performing ensembles again when a golden dragon and a colorful phoenix suddenly flew in and landed on the Phoenix Platform. So Xiao Shi mounting the dragon and Nong Yu riding on the back of the phoenix, they both ascended to the immortal dimension and became an immortal couple.

Like the harmonious play of the 7-stringed zither (*Qin*) and 50-stringed zither with moveable bridges (*Se*), *Sheng* and vertical flute also compose perfect harmonies and thus bring a sweet marriage. There are still some scenic spots in Hua Mountain which were named after this anecdote of Nong Yu playing vertical flute, such as "*Yunü* Peak" and "*Yinfeng* (phoenix drawing) Pavilion", in reminiscence of the beautiful tales.

- 仇英《吹箫引凤图》（明）

Playing Vertical Flute to Draw in the Phoenix by Qiu Ying (Ming Dynasty, 1368-1644)

唢呐

唢呐是中国民族吹管乐器的一种，又称"喇叭"。管身木制，呈圆锥形，上端装有带哨子的铜管，下端套着一个铜制的喇叭口。吹奏时用嘴含住哨子用力吹气，使之振动发声，经过木管身和铜喇叭口的振动及扩音，使唢呐发出高亢嘹亮的声音。唢呐的最大特色在于吹奏者能以嘴巴控制哨子，作出音量、音高、音色的变化，再加上各种技巧的运用，使唢呐可以发出很圆满的滑音，极具表现力。唢呐在中国各地广泛流传，过去多在民间的吹歌会、秧歌会、鼓乐班和地方曲艺、戏曲的伴奏中应用。

唢呐最初是由波斯（今伊朗）传入中国，西晋时期的新疆克孜尔石窟壁画中就已经出现了演

Suo Na Trumpet

Suo Na trumpet is one of ethnic Chinese wind instruments, also known as *La Ba*. The body of its tube is made of wood in a conic shape, the upper part of which is a copper tube with a whistle on it. The lower part is mounted with a bellmouth made of copper. When playing it, the whistle is supposed to be put into one's mouth while air is blown into it in order to make it vibrate and sound out while the wooden body of the tube and the copper bellmouth transmit the vibration and magnify the sound as the distinctive sound of *Suo Na* trumpet is delivered. Generally, the sound of *Suo Na* trumpet is high-pitched and bright. The most distinguished feature of *Suo Na* trumpet lies in the fact that the player can use the mouth to control the whistle and produce a change in volume, pitch and tone. Coupled with other skill applications, *Suo Na* trumpet can deliver accomplished glides in sounds with full expressiveness. *Suo Na* trumpet is pervasively used

• 唢呐
Suo Na Trumpet

奏唢呐的绘画。最晚在16世纪，唢
呐就在中国的民间流传了。不过到了
明代，史籍中才出现了关于唢呐的
记载。明代武将戚继光还曾把唢呐
用于军乐之中。

筚篥

筚篥，又称"笳管"、"头
管"、"管子"，是一种古代的双簧
类乐器。这种乐器以竹为身，以芦苇
为哨，管身开有九个音孔。吹奏时音
色悲凉、深沉，常有如泣如诉之感，

in every corner of China. It used to be present in local blowing songs meeting (*Chui Ge Hui*), rice song gathering (*Yang Ge Hui*), and drumming music band (*Gu Yue Ban*), as well as in the accompanying music of local opera and vocal arts.

Suo Na trumpet was originally carried into China from Persia (now Iran). Among the murals of the Xinjiang Kizil Grottoes in the Western Jin Dynasty (265-317), pictures of *Suo Na* trumpet performance were already illustrated. By the 16th century at the latest, *Suo Na* trumpet had become prevalent in Chinese local society. However, it wasn't until the Ming Dynasty (1368-1644) that *Suo Na* trumpet was recorded in historical literature. The martial general Qi Jiguang of the Ming Dynasty once applied *Suo Na* trumpet in military music.

Double Reed Oboe

Double reed oboe (*Bi Li*), also known as *Jia Guan, Tou Guan or Guan Zi*, is an ancient double reed instrument with a body made of bamboo lined with nine sound holes which uses a reed as a mouthpiece. The music it delivers sounds deep and saddening, like sobbing. That's why it was also called *Bei* (sad) *Li* in ancient times. Double reed oboe

所以古代也称"悲篥"。筚篥于西汉时期流行于古代龟兹（今新疆库车县）地区，大约公元4世纪传入内地。北魏以来开凿的云冈石窟中就有吹筚篥的形象。《旧唐书·音乐志》记载："筚篥，本名悲篥，出于

prevailed in the Western Han Dynasty (206 B.C.-25A.D.) at the ancient place of Qiuci (now Kuche county of Xinjiang), and was carried to the hinterland in around the 4th century. The image of double reed oboe performance was seen in the *Yungang* Grottoes which had been

• 吹筚篥的女子砖雕（五代）
Brick Sculpture of a Female Double Reed Oboe Performer (Five Dynasties, 907-960)

• 吹筚篥的男子砖雕（五代）
Brick Sculpture of a Male Double Reed Oboe Performer (Five Dynasties, 907-960)

尉迟青善吹筚篥

唐代德宗年间，有位名叫尉迟青的军官，非常擅长吹筚篥。当时还有一位筚篥高手，就是名冠幽州的王麻奴。一次，有人要为朋友设宴送行，请王麻奴去演奏，被他拒绝了。于是来人讽刺他说："你和长安的尉迟青还差得远呢！"王麻奴听了不服，就特意来到长安，主动求见尉迟青。二人见面，叙礼完毕，尉迟青请他演奏一曲，王麻奴就吹奏了一首西域乐曲，奏罢累得汗流浃背。接着，尉迟青拿起筚篥，吹奏了同一首曲子，轻松自如，音韵优美。王麻奴心悦诚服，拜而求教。这个故事也说明唐代时来自西域的筚篥在中原广为流行。

Yuchi Qing's Expertise in Double Reed Oboe

During the reign of Dezong in the Tang Dynasty (618-907), an officer named Yuchi Qing was good at playing double reed oboe. At that time, there was a master player of double reed oboe named Wang Manu, who was famous all over Youzhou area. When someone invited Wang Manu to perform at his friend's departure party, he was turned down by Wang. Because of this, someone sarcastically challenged him and said, "You are by far inferior to Yuchi Qing in Chang' an City." Wang was so unconvinced that he made an intentional trip to Chang' an and requested for a meeting with Yuchi Qing. The two met, and after the usual courtesies were exchanged, Yuchi Qing asked Wang to perform for him. Wang played a piece from the western regions and ended up with all sweat. Yuchi Qing then played the same music in a free and relaxed manner as beautifully as it should be. Wang became totally convinced and submissive and asked for Yuchi Qing' s advice. From this story, it is shown that in the Tang Dynasty, though coming from the western regions, double reed oboe had been prevalent in the central plains of China.

中国乐器大家族 The Extended Family of Chinese Musical Instruments

胡中，其声悲。"隋开皇初年（581年），筚篥开始在宫廷乐队中使用，唐宋时期应用颇广，有大筚篥、小筚篥、双筚篥、桃皮筚篥等形制。到了明代，筚篥管身改用木制，音色变得更为淳厚。明清两代，筚篥更多被称为"管子"，广泛流行于民间。

cut since the Northern Wei Dynasty (386-534). In *Annals of Music* in the *Old Book of Tang*, it is stated that "Double reed oboe originally named *Bei*(sad) *Li*, came from the northern barbarian tribes with saddening sound." In the first year of Kaihuang Period (around 581) in the Sui Dynasty (581-618), double reed oboe began to be played in court music bands.

笙

　　笙是一种有两千多年历史的簧管乐器，其构造是将铜制的簧片装在若干竹管下端，将这些竹管插在一个木制或铜制的带有吹孔的笙斗上。吹时用手指按着竹管下端所开的孔，使簧片与管中气柱发生共鸣

- 吹笙女子砖雕（五代）
Brick Sculpture of a Female Playing *Sheng* (Five Dynasties, 907-960)

The Tang Dynasty (618-907) and Song Dynasty (960-1279) had seen extensive usage of double reed oboe with various shapes such as big double reed oboe, small double reed oboe, dual double reed oboe and peach tree branch double reed oboe. In the Ming Dynasty (1368-1644), the material for the tube of double reed oboe was changed to wood and the sound became plainer and deeper. In the Ming Dynasty and Qing Dynasty, double reed oboe was widely known as *Guan Zi* and popularly used in local societies.

Sheng

Sheng is a reed-pipe instrument with a history of more than 2,000 years. Structurally, a copper reed is installed at the bottom end of a number of bamboo pipes which are inserted into a wood or copper box, called *Sheng Dou*, with a blowing hole. When playing, the player's finger tips cover the holes at the bottom of the bamboo pipes to produce resonance between the reed and the air contained within the pipes to send out the sound. *Sheng* has a bright and sweet tone, with a crisp and transparent high pitch, soft and plump alto, and a loud, deep and full bass. Among the Chinese traditional wind instruments, *Sheng* is the only one

• 吹笙引凤画像砖（南朝）

传说西周时周灵王的太子名叫王子乔，喜好吹笙，作凤凰鸣，乐声真切，以至引来凤凰飞舞。

Brick Painting of *Sheng* Performance to Draw in the Phoenix (Southern Dynasty, 420-589)

Legend has it that Wang Ziqiao, prince of King Ling in the Western Zhou Dynasty (1046 B.C.-771 B.C.), embraced the hobby of playing *Sheng*. He could make it sound like a real phoenix crying, so that the phoenix was drawn in.

• 伎乐俑（唐）

Figurine of Musical Dance (Tang Dynasty, 618-907)

而发出乐音。笙的音色明亮甜美，高音清脆透明，中音柔和丰满，低音浑厚低沉，音量较大。在中国传统吹管乐器中，笙是唯一能够吹出和声的乐器，在与其他乐器合奏的时候，能起到调和乐队音色、丰富

that can be played chords. When played in an ensemble with other instruments, it can effectively adjust the tone of the band and set the acoustic in full play.

The *Sheng Dou* of the earliest *Sheng* was made from a gourd. That's why it has been classified in the "eight sounds"

传统乐器
Traditional Chinese Musical Instruments

● 吹笙乐伎纹玉带板（南宋）
Jade Belt Linked to Board with *Sheng*-playing Dancer (Southern Song Dynasty, 1127-1279)

乐队音响的作用。

　　最早的笙，其笙斗是用葫芦制成，所以在"八音"分类法中归于"匏"这一类。1978年，曾侯乙墓出土了2400多年前的几支匏笙，这是中国目前发现的最早的笙。春秋战国时期，笙已非常流行，是为声乐伴奏的主要乐器，同时也可用来合奏或独奏。南北朝到隋唐时期，笙在当时盛行的燕乐、清乐、西凉乐、高丽乐、龟兹乐中均被采用。早期的笙管为竹制，后来改为铜制。明清时期，民间流传的笙种类繁多，形制大小各不相同。

under the category of "gourd". In 1978, several gourd *Sheng* from 2,400 years ago were unearthed from the Tomb of Marquis Yi of Zeng. So far, they are the earliest *Sheng* ever discovered in China. In the Spring and Autumn and Warring States Period (770 B.C.-221 B.C.), *Sheng* had already been quite popular, being performed not only as major accompaniment of vocal music but also in solos and ensembles. From the Southern and Northern Dynasties (386-589) through the Sui Dynasty (581-618) and Tang Dynasty (618-907), *Sheng* had been widely applied in popular music such as *Yan* music, *Qing* music, *Xiliang* music, Goryeo music and *Qiuci* music. Earlier *Sheng* pipes were made of bamboo. The material was later changed to copper. During the Ming Dynasty and Qing Dynasty (1368-1911), a great variety of *Sheng* appeared in different sizes and forms.

● 现代的笙
Modern *Sheng*

滥竽充数

竽也是中国古代的一种吹奏乐器，其形制和发声原理都和笙很相近，不过体形较大，而且竽管数量也比笙要多。据史料记载，汉代以前的竽曾多达三十六管，后来逐渐减为二十二管。战国时期，竽和笙在宫廷乐队中并存，而且比笙更受重用。中国有个家喻户晓的成语——"滥竽充数"，它讲的是在战国时期的齐国，齐宣王喜欢听吹竽，而且常常要三百人一起吹。有个不会吹竽的南郭先生，向齐宣王吹嘘自己吹竽技艺非常高超。齐宣王便将他编入乐队之中，给他丰厚的待遇。每逢演奏的时候，南郭先生就捧着竽混在队伍中装腔作势，一直没有露出破绽。不久，齐宣王死了，他的儿子齐湣王继承了王位。齐湣王也很喜欢听吹竽，但他喜欢听独奏，南郭先生就只好灰溜溜地逃走了。滥竽充数这个成语用来比喻没有真正的才干，而混在行家里面充数的人或现象。

Lan Yu Chong Shu (Filling in the unqualified one to make up the number)

Yu was also an ancient Chinese wind instrument whose form and sounding principles were very similar to those of *Sheng* except that it is bigger in size and has more pipes than *Sheng*. According to historic records, the *Yu* instrument before the Han Dynasty (206 B.C.-220 A.D.) might have as many as 36 pipes though it was gradually reduced to 22 in number. In the Warring States Period (475 B.C.-221 B.C.), *Yu* was paired up with *Sheng* in a court musical bands and enjoyed more importance than *Sheng*. The well-known Chinese idiom *Lan Yu Chong Shu* came from the story where in the state of Qi during the Warring States Period, King Xuan favored the music of *Yu* and enjoyed it being played by a band of 300 players. A man named Nan Guo, who was awkward at the art of *Yu*, boasted to King Xuan of his high expertise in the art until the King finally enrolled him in the band and paid him a very good salary. Every time when the band was performing, Nan Guo would hold his *Yu* and blend in with the other players in successful mimicry without being exposed. Before long, the King died and his son Min succeeded to the throne. King Min enjoyed *Yu* music too, but preferred it in the solo form. As a result, Mr. Nan Guo could not do anything but escape secretly. Henceforth, the idiom of *Lan Yu Chong Shu* is used to describe either a person in question or for a matter where someone with no genuine talent mixes in a lineup of professionals to increase its number.

- 马王堆汉墓出土的竽

Yu Unearthed from the *Mawangdui* Tomb of Han Dynasty (206 B.C.-220 A.D.)

中国乐器大家族 The Extended Family of Chinese Musical Instruments

芦笙

芦笙是中国苗族、侗族、瑶族、水族、仡佬族、傣族、布朗族等民族的一种吹奏乐器，流行于贵州、广西、云南、湖南等少数民族聚居的地区。据记载，芦笙已有3000多年的历史。

各地芦笙大小不一，管的数目也不尽相同，较常见的是六管芦笙。其构造是用六根长短不一的竹管，分成二排插入木制的笙斗；每根管的根部各装一个铜质簧片；管的下端各开一个小孔，吹奏时手指按孔发音，以单音奏旋律，同时发出两个以上的和音做伴奏。

自古以来，芦笙的吹奏都要配合舞蹈，边吹边舞。苗族、侗族、

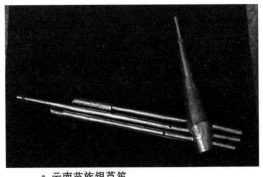

• 云南苗族银芦笙
Silver *Lu Sheng* of Miao People, Yunnan Province

Lu Sheng

Lu Sheng is a wind instrument played in the ethnic groups of Miao, Dong, Yao, Shui, Gelao, Dai and Bulang. It prevails in the areas inhabited by these ethnic minorities in Guizhou, Guangxi, Yunnan, Hunan and others. According to records, *Lu Sheng* has a history of over 3,000 years.

The size of *Lu Sheng* differs from place to place. The number of pipes differs as well, though the common type is the six-pipe *Lu Sheng*, with six tubes of different lengths set in two rows and inserted into a wood *Sheng Dou*. Each pipe has a copper reed at its bottom. A small hole at the lower end of each pipe is supposed to be covered by fingertips to give different sounds. Monophonic rhythm is played with the accompaniment of two or more summation tones.

Since the very beginning, *Lu Sheng* players have performed the instrument in combination with dancing. During celebrations, Miao people, Dong people and Yao people will always hold *Tiao* (jump) *Lu Sheng* events, where young lads blow the *Lu Sheng* while girls dressed up in ethnic costumes will follow them and form a circle. The young

瑶族等各族人在喜庆的日子常常举行"跳芦笙"的活动，一般是小伙子吹芦笙，而姑娘们身着民族盛装跟随其后，围成一个圆圈。吹笙的小伙子边吹边随着节奏跳舞，忽前忽后，欢喜雀跃，姑娘们根据旋律做出各种舞姿，场面颇为壮观。

players will dance to the rhythm of their own music, stepping to and fro in joyful leaps, while girls will dance in various poses in tune with the music, making the scene a magnificent spectacle.

● 贵州苗寨的芦笙舞（图片提供:FOTOE）
Lu Sheng Dance in the Miao Village, Guizhou Province

芦笙的传说

在苗族的神话传说中，在远古时代，苗族人的祖先告且和告当造出了日月，又从天公那里盗来谷种撒到地里，可惜谷子收成很差。为了解忧，告且和告当从山上砍了六根白苦竹扎成一束，放在口中一吹，发出了奇特的乐声。奇怪的是，地里的稻谷在乐声中长得十分茂盛，当年获得了大丰收。从此以后，苗家每逢喜庆的日子都要吹起芦笙，载歌载舞。实际上早在唐代，进京朝贡的少数民族就曾带着芦笙到宫廷中演奏过，得到了朝廷官员的高度赞赏。

the Legend of *Lu Sheng*

A mythological tale of Miao people goes like this: once upon a time in the remote antiquity, the ancestors of Miao, Gao Qie and Gao Dang, who created the sun and the moon, stole the seeds of grains from heaven and spread them on earth. Unfortunately, the grains didn't grow well. To pass the hard time, Gao Qie and Gao Dang bundled up the six white, bitter bamboo rods which they had chopped down and brought back from the mountain, and put them in their mouths while blowing them. The men played such wonderful music that all the grains in the earth began to grow with the music. They reaped a good harvest that year. Ever since then, it has been a necessity for every Miao family to play *Lu Sheng* and dance with the music on any occasion that calls for celebration. In fact, as early as the Tang Dynasty (618-907), whenever the ethnic groups came to pay tribute to the imperial family in the capital, they would bring their *Lu Sheng* and play the instruments in the court. They were highly praised by the imperial officials.

葫芦丝

葫芦丝是一种少数民族的吹奏乐器，发源于云南省德宏傣族景颇族自治州，主要流行于傣族、阿昌族、佤族、德昂族和布朗族聚居的云南德宏、临沧地区，富有浓郁的地方色彩。这种乐器用半截小葫芦作为音箱，以三根长短不一的竹管并排插在葫芦下端，嵌有铜质簧

Cucurbit Flute

Cucurbit flute (*Hu Lu Si*) is a wind instrument of ethnic minorities. It originated in Dehong Dai and Jingpo Autonomous Prefecture in Yunnan Province, and is popularized in Dehong and Lincang areas of Yunnan Province, inhabited by the tribes of Dai, Achang, Wa, De'ang, and Bulang. It has very dense regionalism. Cucurbit flute uses

● 傣族泼水节
Water-sprinkling Festival of Dai People

片，中间较长的一根竹管开七孔。吹奏时口吹葫芦细端，指按中间竹管的音孔，在奏出旋律的同时，左右两根竹管同时发出固定的单音，与旋律构成和音。其音乐轻柔细腻，圆润质朴，极富表现力。

葫芦丝的历史十分悠久，其渊源可追溯到先秦时期。关于葫芦丝的起源，傣族民间还流传着这样一个传说：很久以前，一次山洪暴发，一位傣家小伙子抱起一个大葫芦，闯过惊涛骇浪，救出自己的心

half a gourd as the sound box with three different-length and copper-reed bamboo tubes inserted under the gourd. The longest bamboo tube is placed in the middle and has seven holes. When playing, the mouth blows air into the small opening of the gourd while the fingers cover the sound holes of the middle bamboo pipe. While music is being played, the other two pipes deliver fixed monophonic sounds and blend with the melody into ensembles. The music it plays sounds soft and delicate, round and plain, with abundant expressiveness.

● 葫芦丝
Cucurbit Flute

上人。他忠贞不渝的爱情感动了佛祖，佛祖给葫芦装上了管子，小伙子吹出了美妙的乐声，顿时大地鲜花盛开，孔雀开屏，祝愿这对情侣吉祥幸福。从此葫芦丝在傣族人家世代相传。

巴乌

巴乌属于簧管乐器，也叫"把乌"，流行于云南省彝、苗、哈尼等民族中。巴乌用竹管制成，有八个指孔（前七后一），在吹口处置一尖舌形铜制簧片，演奏时横吹上端，振动簧片发声。巴乌音量较小，但音色柔美，很像一对恋人在窃窃私语，低诉衷肠。所以每到晚间，彝族、哈尼族、苗族青年在谈恋爱时，常用它抒发自己的衷肠，传递爱慕之情。

As a time-honored instrument, cucurbit flute dates back to the pre-Qin period (before 221 B.C.). Dai people have a legend concerning the origin of cucurbit flute: once upon a time when a serious torrential flood broke out, a young Dai man survived the torrents of the horrible tides of water by holding onto a big gourd and rescued his lover. Buddha was deeply moved by this young man's faithful love and inserted a pipe into the gourd for him to blow. As soon as the young man played the wonderful music, all the flowers around him bloomed and peacocks joyfully displayed their glorious tails to congratulate the couple for their good luck and happiness. Ever since then, the cucurbit flute has been passed down in Dai households from one generation to another.

Ba Wu

Ba Wu, also known as Ba'r Wu, is a reed wind instrument, popularized in the ethnic groups of Yi, Miao and Hani in Yunnan Province. *Ba Wu* is made of a bamboo pipe with eight finger holes

• 巴乌
Ba Wu

• 演奏巴乌的彝族少女 （图片提供：FOTOE）
Young Girl of Yi Ethnic Group Performing
Ba Wu

(seven in the front and the other on the back) and a tongue-like copper reed in the mouthpiece. Air is blown transversely onto the reed for vibration. Though it has a small volume, the sweet and soft timbre makes it sound like a pair of lovers whispering softly. In the evening, the youths of Yi, Hani, and Miao who are in love always make use of *Ba Wu* to express their feelings and confide their love.

巴乌的传说

　　哈尼族民间流传着关于巴乌的一个古老故事：很早很早以前，在云南红河南岸的哀牢山区，有一位纯洁、美丽、善良的哈尼族姑娘梅乌，她与英俊、勇敢、勤劳的小伙子巴冲相爱。他俩发誓要永世相伴，寨子里的人无不羡慕他们。这事被深山里的魔鬼知道了，它趁人们歌舞时，驾着一阵狂风把姑娘掠走了，硬逼着姑娘和他成亲。姑娘坚贞不屈，始终一言不发。魔鬼恼羞成怒，凶残地割去了她的舌头，并将她扔进了深山老林。姑娘怀念着心上的恋人，整天徘徊在山林之间。一天，树林里的仙鸟衔来了姑娘的舌头和一截竹子，让姑娘把舌头放进竹管里，告诉她"竹子会帮助你说话"。于是姑娘吹响了竹子，发出了优美的乐音，表达出了对恋人的思念和对魔鬼的控诉。乐音传到巴冲耳边，小伙子历尽艰险，把姑娘救了回来。后来人们给这件会说话的乐器取名为"巴乌"。从此，巴乌就在哈尼山寨世代流传。

The Legend of *Ba Wu*

There is a very old folk tale circulating in the Hani tribe: A very long time ago, in the Ailao Mountains on the south bank of Red River in Yunnan Province, a chaste, beautiful and kind Hani girl, Mei Wu, was in love with a handsome, brave, and hard-working young man named Ba Chong. They promised each other they would keep each other's company for the rest of their lives and all the people in the village were envious of them. However, the devil in the remote mountains learned of this and took the chance, while all the villagers were dancing, to kidnap Mei Wu and carry her away in a strong gust of wind, forcing her to marry him. The faithful and unyielding girl kept silent toward the devil. Being shamed into a rage, the devil brutally cut off her tongue and threw her into the deep woods of the remotest mountain. The girl kept lingering in the woods, missing her beloved Ba Chong. One day, a fairy bird flew to her bearing her cut-off tongue and a bamboo stick in its beak. It put the cut-off tongue into the bamboo stick and told her, "The bamboo shall help you talk." As the girl blew air into the stick and sounded the bamboo pipe, it sent out beautiful music and interpreted her longing for her beloved one as well as her complaints against the devil. The music was heard by Ba Chong, who endured a series of difficulties before finally rescuing her back. The speaking instrument was later named *Ba Wu* and has been passed down in the Hani villages through several generations.

• 美丽的哈尼族姑娘
Beautiful Hani Girls

> 拉弦乐器

拉弦乐器是用装在细竹弓子上的马尾摩擦琴弦，使之振动发音的一种乐器。中国常见的拉弦乐器包括二胡、板胡、高胡、中胡、革胡、四胡等。

二胡

中国最早的拉弦乐器始于唐代，包括流行于北方的奚琴和轧筝。宋元时期，随着戏曲、曲艺等民间艺术的发展，伴奏乐器也随之发展起来。其中最主要的乐器是源自蒙古和西域的马尾胡琴，它与之前的奚琴、轧筝融合，演变出新颖的胡琴。这一乐器标志着中国拉弦乐器走向成熟。明清时期，由于地方戏唱腔风格需要，胡琴又逐渐分化，出现了配合秦腔、豫剧的板

> Bowed String Instrument

The bowed string instrument uses horsetail on a slim bamboo bow to rub the strings and cause a vibration which makes the instrument emit sounds. The most common Chinese bowed string instruments include *Er Hu* (two-stringed fiddle), *Ban Hu* (two-stringed fiddle with a coconut resonator and wooden face), *Gao Hu* (two-stringed fiddle with higher pitch than *Er Hu*), *Zhong Hu* (two-stringed fiddle with lower pitch than *Er Hu*), *Ge Hu* (four-stringed bass instrument) and *Si Hu* (four-stringed fiddle with strings tuned in pairs).

Er Hu

The earliest Chinese bowed string instruments, including *Xi* fiddle and *Ya* bowed-zither which are popular in north China, can be dated back to the Tang Dynasty (618-907). In the Song

Dynasty (960-1279) and Yuan Dynasty (1206-1368), accompaniment instruments grew rapidly as the development of local operas and vocal arts progressed. Among them, the most dominant one was the horsetail fiddle, which originated in Mongolia and the western regions. It was combined with the previous *Xi* fiddle and *Ya* bowed-zither into the innovative form of fiddle (*Hu Qin*). Fiddle fully marks the maturity of Chinese bowed string instruments. During the Ming Dynasty (1368-1644) and Qing Dynasty (1644-1911), in response to the various demands for the highly-styled singing tunes of local operas, the uniform fiddle began to be differentiated into such forms as *Ban Hu* for *Qin Qiang* and *Yu* opera, *Jing Hu* and *Jing Er Hu* for Beijing opera and *Han* opera, *Zhui Hu* for *Zhui Zi* opera of Henan Province, *Gao Hu* for *Yue* opera of Guangdong Province, *Ye Hu* for *Chao* opera, and *Si Hu* for Mongolian storytelling.

Er Hu (two-stringed fiddle) is the most representative member of the large family of fiddle. Its simple structure is composed of the sound box, pillar, skin, tuning pegs, strings, bow, *Qian Jin* (a loop of string acting as a nut) and bridge. The bow hair of the bow is placed

• 王树榖《弄胡琴图》（清）
Playing Fiddle by Wang Shuhu (Qing Dynasty, 1644-1911)

胡，京剧、汉剧需要的京胡、京二胡，河南坠子需要的坠胡，广东粤剧需要的高胡，潮剧需要的椰胡，蒙古说唱用的四胡等等各种弓弦乐器。

　　二胡是胡琴大家族中最具代表性的成员之一。它的构造比较简单，由琴筒、琴杆、琴皮、弦轴、琴轴，又名"琴轸"，有上下两个，起调整音高的作用，上下琴轴各张一根琴弦，即较粗的内弦和较细的外弦。这也是"二胡"名称的由来。

Pegs, also known as *Qin Zhen*, refer to the upper and lower pegs functioning to tune up the pitch. Each of them is holding a string, with the thicker string in the inside and the thinner one in the outside. These two strings gave rise to the instrument name *Er* (two) *Hu*.

琴杆是支撑琴弦的重要支柱，顶端为琴头，上部装有两个弦轴，下端插入琴筒。琴头呈弯脖形，也有雕刻成龙头或其他形状的。

Pillar refers to the main pillar to support the strings. Its top is the head with two tuning pegs; its bottom is inserted into the sound box. The head is a little bent like a neck, and sometimes sculptured in the image of a dragon head or others.

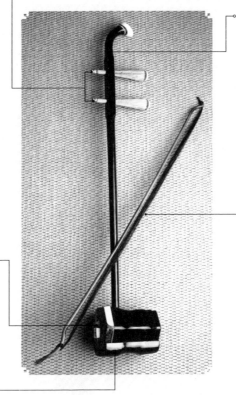

弓子，由弓杆和弓毛两部分组成。弓杆一端装有活螺丝（弓鱼），可调整弓毛松紧度。弓毛多用马尾制成。

Bow is composed of bow stem and bow hair. At one end of the bow is an adjustable screw which serves to adjust the tension of the bow hair. The bow hair is mostly from the horse tail.

琴码，作用是把弦的振动传导到蟒皮上，材料有木、竹、金属和纸等。

Bridge works to transmit the vibration of the string to the python skin. It is made of such materials as wood, bamboo, metal, paper, and so on.

琴筒，琴弓擦弦后振动琴皮发音的共鸣体，一般用紫檀木或红木制作，形状有六角形、八角形、圆形等。琴筒前口蒙皮，一般为蟒皮；后口有雕花音窗。

Sound box is the resonator body where the friction of the bow and strings vibrates the skin to generate sounds. It is usually made of rosewood or redwood in hexagonal, octagonal or round shapes. The front of the box is covered with a layer of skin usually from python, while the back side is a sculptured sound window.

• 二胡（图片提供：全景正片）
Er Hu

琴弦、弓子、千斤、琴码等部分组成。弓子的弓毛夹于两根琴弦之间。演奏时，左手按弦，右手拉弓，使弓毛与琴弦摩擦而发音。二胡发出的声音极富歌唱性，宛如人的歌声，既能演奏得细腻柔美、深沉抒情，又能表现得热烈欢快、激情奔放。

between the two strings. When playing, the left hand presses the string while the right hand pulls the bow to generate friction between the bow hair and the strings to produce sounds. The music of *Er Hu* is impregnated with vocal effects in proximity to the human singing voice. It can play either soft and tender strains or deep and lyric songs, while being capable of a heated, jubilant feeling, as well as excited and passionate emotions.

● 苏州留园内演奏二胡的姑娘
A Young Girl Playing *Er Hu* in *Liu Garden*, Suzhou

瞎子阿炳与《二泉映月》

阿炳是二胡艺术史上最负盛名的民间音乐家，原名华彦钧，生于清光绪十九年（1893年），江苏无锡人。他因中年后双目失明，人称"瞎子阿炳"。

阿炳从小学习多种民间乐器的演奏，具有很高的艺术造诣。他在20世纪40年代创作的二胡独奏曲《二泉映月》，是中国二胡曲中的代表作。"二泉"即江苏无锡的惠山泉，其有"天下第二泉"之称。作者以《二泉映月》为曲名，表现了一个刚直不阿的盲艺人在泉清月冷的晚上，孤独一人用乐器诉说人世不平和生活艰辛的凄切情景。乐曲通过对月夜景色的描绘，抒发了作者内心无限深邃的感情，倾诉了那个时代人们所承受的苦难，以及精神上的痛苦。作品同时又表达了人们对美好生活的向往。阿炳把他的悲、他的恨、他的爱，全都融在《二泉映月》那深情的旋律中。全曲撼人心弦，感人肺腑。日本著名音乐指挥家小泽征尔在听了这首乐曲后，不无感慨地说："如此断肠之曲，我不配来指挥，只配跪下来倾听。"

● 瞎子阿炳拉二胡雕像
Sculpture of Abing the Blind Playing *Er Hu*

Abing the Blind and *Er Quan Ying Yue (The Moon over a Fountain)*

Abing, originally named Hua Yanjun, is a native of Wuxi City Jiangsu Province. He was born in 1893, the 19th year of the reign of Emperor Guangxu in Qing Dynasty (1644-1911), and is the most famous folk musician in the art history of *Er Hu*. He was blind at middle age, and hence called "Abing the Blind". Abing had been studying multiple local instruments since his childhood, and had scored very high achievements in the art. In the 40s of the 20th century, he created the *Er Hu* solo masterpiece, *Er Quan Ying Yue (The Moon Over a Fountain)*. Er Quan refers to the Huishan Fountain of Wuxi in Jiangsu Province, known as "the Second Fountain of China". The author titled the piece as such in order to display a plaintive scene that a lonely blind musician with integrity using the instrument to narrate the miserable tales of difficult life in an unjust world by a clear fountain at a night with a bright moon. Through the descriptions of the night scene under the moon, the music confides the unfathomable feelings in the heart of the author, and expresses the sufferings that people at that time had borne as well as the afflictions on their minds. In the mean time, it also exposes people's hope for a good and beautiful life. Abing had infused his sadness, his grievance and his love into the deep passion of the *Er Quan Ying Yue* melody. The whole piece has blended the scene and the feeling in fusion and pinched people's mind chord in a strongly touching manner. After hearing this musical piece, the prestigious Japanese music conductor, Seiji Osawa, exclaimed that "'heartbroken feeling is a picturesque word for it."

● 被称为 "天下第二泉" 的无锡惠山泉
Huishan Fountain in Wuxi: Honored as the "Second Fountain of China"

板胡

板胡又名"梆胡"、"秦胡"等，是伴随戏曲梆子腔的出现，在胡琴的基础上产生的乐器。大约在明末清初，板胡随着梆子腔的兴起而流行，后为多种地方戏曲和曲艺所吸收，如河北梆子、评剧、吕剧、豫剧、晋剧、秦腔、蒲剧、兰州鼓子、道情及南方婺剧、绍兴大板等，也用于南北吹打乐、鼓吹乐的合奏。

板胡的结构绝大部分和二胡相同，二者最主要的区别在于琴筒。板胡琴筒的前口不像二胡那样蒙蟒皮，而是用桐木板，这是板胡发音的关键。板胡的音色特别清澈响亮，富有乡土气息，鲜明突出，在表现高亢激昂、热烈欢腾、泼辣

• 板胡
Ban Hu

Ban Hu

Ban Hu (two-stringed fiddle with a coconut resonator and wooden face), otherwise called *Bang Hu*, or *Qin Hu*, came to existence along with the opera of *Bang Zi* tone on the basis of fiddle. Around the end of Ming Dynasty (1368-1644) and the beginning of Qing Dynasty (1644-1911), *Ban Hu* became popular along with *Bang Zi* tone, and was later absorbed by various local operas and vocal arts such as *Bang Zi* of Hebei Province, *Ping* opera, *Lü* opera, *Yu* opera, *Jin* opera, *Qin Qiang*, *Pu* opera, *Gu Zi* of Lanzhou, *Dao Qing*, as well as *Wu* opera in southern China and Shaoxing *Da Ban* and the like. It is also used in the ensembles of southern and northern *Chui Da* music, and *Gu Chui* music.

Structurally, *Ban Hu* is the same with *Er Hu* in most parts except the biggest difference in the sound box. Instead of a python skin like *Er Hu*, the front opening of sound box of *Ban Hu* is covered with a thin paulownia board as the key for sounding. The tone of *Ban Hu* is crisp and sonorous with unique and strong local flavor and distinctive bright timbre, being highly expressive in high-pitched excitement, heated jubilant atmosphere,

奔放的情绪方面最富有特色。在演奏技巧上，除一般拉弦乐器常用技法外，还有滑音、双音、弹弦、按弦等技法。

and shrewish and outbound emotions. In addition to the common bowed string skills, its playing incorporates such skills as glide, double tones, string plucking, string pressing, and so on.

梆子腔

梆子腔是中国戏曲的四大声腔系统之一，因以硬木梆子击节而得名。梆子腔于明末起源于今陕西省境内，广泛流行于甘肃、宁夏、青海、新疆等地。演出时以硬木梆子击节，以不同形制的板胡为主奏乐器，唱调为上下句式，多以华彩流畅的花腔乐句为辅，整个音乐风格高亢激越，悲壮粗犷。如今地方戏中的陕西秦腔、山西梆子、河北梆子、河南豫剧等，均属梆子腔。

Bang Zi Tone

Bang Zi tone is one of the four vocal tune systems of Chinese opera, named after the hardwooden stick (*Bang Zi*) used for the musical beats. *Bang Zi* tone originated in ancient Shaanxi Province in the end of the Ming Dynasty (1368-1644), and prevailed in Gansu, Ningxia, Qinghai, Xinjiang, and other places. In performance, the hardwood clapper is used for beat, and different forms of *Ban Hu* serve as the major instruments. The vocal is based on couplets and coupled with fluent and colorful musical sentences of coloratura, making the overall music style intense, sonorous, solemnly stirring, and unrestrained. Currently in local operas, there are Shaanxi *Qin Qiang*, Shanxi *Bang Zi*, Hebei *Bang Zi*, Henan *Yu* opera, etc., all of which belong to *Bang Zi* tone.

• 山西梆子的演出 (图片提供：FOTOE)
Performance of Shanxi *Bang Zi*

京胡

18世纪末，随着中国传统戏曲中最受欢迎的剧种——京剧的形成，京胡也在传统胡琴的基础上改制而成，至今已有200多年的历史，一直是京剧的主要伴奏乐器。

最早的京胡琴杆很短，琴筒也很小，用软弓（即弓毛松软）拉奏，被称为"软弓京胡"。19世纪以后，京胡逐渐开始用硬弓拉奏，琴杆、琴筒不断加大，京胡也逐渐在各地流行起来，特别是在北京地区尤为盛行。

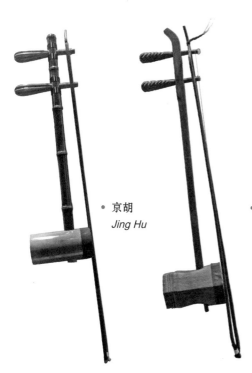

● 京胡
Jing Hu

Jing Hu

At the end of 18th century, as the most popular Chinese traditional opera, Beijing opera, was formed, *Jing Hu* came into being as well on the basis of traditional fiddle. For more than 200 hundred years, *Jing Hu* has been the major accompanying instrument of Beijing opera.

With a very short pillar and a very small sound box, the earliest *Jing Hu* used soft bow (soft bow hair) for playing, and hence was also called soft-bow *Jing Hu*. Since the 19th century, *Jing Hu* began to adopt the hard bow for playing, and enlarge both parts of the pillar and sound box. It became popularized especially in Beijing. Unlike the *Er Hu*, *Jing Hu* has its sound box and pillar made of bamboo. It has smaller sound box and unfixed tuning strings, with high-pitched tone but

中国乐器大家族 The Extended Family of Chinese Musical Instruments

● 京二胡
京二胡是在二胡的基础上改造而成的乐器，琴体比京胡稍大，比二胡稍小，音色圆润而浑厚，音量洪大，主要用于京剧伴奏。

Jing Er Hu
Jing Er Hu is an innovation on the basis of *Er Hu* with a body a little bigger than *Jing Hu* but a little smaller than *Er Hu*. It has full and deep timbre with sonorous volume, and is mostly used as accompanying instrument in Beijing opera.

京胡与二胡的异同在于，琴筒和琴杆都为竹质，琴筒较小，音高、域窄，定弦不固定。京胡演奏时音质明亮，发音刚劲有力，在合奏中有穿透力。京胡大多用于京剧伴奏，与唱腔很贴切，在节奏感和力度上给唱腔以有力的支撑和补充。

narrow sound gamut. When performed, *Jing Hu* stands out in bright quality, and strong and solid sounds with penetrating power in ensembles. It is mostly applied in accompaniment with Beijing opera, for it attaches very close to the singing tunes and can support and supplement the singing tune with distinctive sense of beats and strength.

京胡与光绪皇帝

清朝光绪年间（1875-1908），皇宫里从慈禧太后到皇室子弟都十分喜欢京剧，而且几乎个个都成了行家里手。演艺精湛的京剧演员常常被召进宫去，乐师也一同随去伴奏。当时有个叫孙佐臣的京胡演奏名家也常常被召进宫表演。他有一把很好的胡琴，

• 光绪帝像
Portrait of Emperor Guangxu
(1871-1908)

在行家眼里堪称千金难换的宝贝。同样十分喜爱京剧和京胡的光绪皇帝知道孙佐臣有这么一把上等好琴，就下令请孙佐臣进宫演奏。悠扬的胡琴声回荡在耳边，光绪帝陶醉了，他闭着眼睛，一边打着节拍一边听。当胡琴声停下来时，光绪突然睁眼，马上朝孙佐臣走去。孙佐臣还没来得及反应，胡琴已经被光绪帝拿走了。

孙佐臣向来爱琴如命，尤其是对这把上等胡琴更是珍爱有加。光绪把胡琴拿走了之后，孙佐臣便一病不起。慈禧太后看到宫中的好几次京剧伴奏都没有孙佐臣，心生疑惑。当知道事情的来龙去脉后，她马上命光绪把胡琴还给了孙佐臣。不过，光绪依旧喜欢胡琴，喜欢京剧。当慈禧太后把他关在瀛台后，戏曲弦歌就是他的玩伴，直到生命的最后。

Jing Hu and Emperor Guangxu

During the reign of Guangxu (1875-1908) in Qing Dynasty, the imperial family members from the Empress Dowager Cixi to the younger generations were all Beijing opera lovers and even experts, too. Those Beijing opera performers with excellent skills were often summoned into the palace for performances, and their musicians were in the company as well. At that time, there was a famous *Jing Hu* player, Sun Zuochen, who was often called upon to perform in the palace. Sun had a very good fiddle, which was a valuable treasure in the eyes of experts. After Emperor Guangxu, who was also very fond of Beijing opera and *Jing Hu*, learned of this, he ordered Sun to perform in the palace. As the melodious sounds floating in the ears, Emperor Guangxu was intoxicated, with eyes closed and clapping in keeping with the beats. As the music of the fiddle stopped, Emperor Guangxu suddenly opened his eyes, made his way to Sun Zuochen, and snapped away his fiddle before he was able to react.

Sun Zuochen had always held his fiddle dear, and he had such a special fondness of this exquisite fiddle the Emperor took away that he finally got sick. When the Empress Dowagers Cixi noticed Sun's absence in the following court performances, she felt things were fishy. After she learned what had happened, she ordered the Emperor to return the fiddle to Sun Zuochen. Whatever had happened, Guangxu's favor of fiddle and Beijing opera had never dwindled. Even during the time when he was imprisoned in *Yingtai*, the string music and opera was still his hobbies till the end of his life.

马头琴

马头琴是中国蒙古族的传统拉弦乐器，因其琴杆上端雕有马头而得名。马头琴由唐宋时期拉弦乐器奚琴发展演变而来，历史十分悠久。在元代，马头琴已开始在民间流传。明清时期，马头琴更被编入了宫廷乐队。

传统的马头琴多为马头琴演奏者就地取材自制而成，所以用料和规格尺寸很不一致。它最突出的特

Horsehead Fiddle

Horsehead fiddle (*Ma Tou Qin*) is a traditional bowed string instrument of a Chinese ethnic group, the Mongol people. It is named because of the sculptured horsehead on the pillar. Horsehead fiddle has a time-honored history and is developed from *Xi* fiddle, the bowed string instruments in the Tang Dynasty (618-907) and Song Dynasty (960-1279). In the Yuan Dynasty (1206-1368), horsehead fiddle had begun to gain popularity in local societies. In Ming and

● 马头琴
Horsehead Fiddle

点是，琴箱用硬木制成，形状呈梯形，而且两面都蒙有马皮、牛皮或羊皮的皮膜；琴杆细长，琴弓和琴弦都用马尾制成，演奏时马尾弓摩擦马尾弦，这在中外拉弦乐器中都是极为独特的。琴师演奏马头琴时一般采用坐姿，将琴箱夹于两腿中间，琴杆偏向左侧。由于马头琴的琴弓不像二胡那样夹在两弦中间，而是直接从前面摩擦琴弦，所以可以像西式提琴那样奏出双音，增加

Qing periods (1368-1911), horsehead fiddle was further incorporated into the court musical bands.

Traditionally, the player of horsehead fiddle would pick up whatever the material available to construct the instrument. Therefore, there is no conformity in the use of material or the size. However, the most outstanding feature of it is in the sound box, which is made of hardwood in trapezoid shape with both sides covered with the membrane of horsehide, cowhide or sheep skin. The pillar is slender; both the bow hair and string are from horse tails. When played, the horsetail bow hair is rubbing the strings made of horsetail hairs, which is another special characteristic of the instrument among all the bowed string instruments within and without China. Usually the musician sits to play it and places the sound box between the legs with the pillar slightly slanting to the left side. Unlike the *Er Hu*, the bow of the horsehead fiddle is not inserted between the two strings; therefore, it can rub the strings in the front and produce double tones like the violin with increased expressiveness.

The sweet, full, expansive and melodious tone of horsehead fiddle

了表现力。

马头琴发音甘美、浑厚、悠扬、动听，善于演奏柔和细腻的乐曲，特别适于表现悠长辽阔的旋律，能够准确的表达出蒙古人的生活，如辽阔的草原、呼啸的狂风、奔腾的马蹄声、欢乐的牧歌以及悲伤的心情等。

serves well for soft and delicate music, especially for the long-drawn and expansive rhythm tune to express the life of Mongol people with a view of the vast grassland, the gusty wind, the saddened feelings, the hoof-beat of galloping horses, the joyful pastoral songs, and so on.

苏和与马头琴

传说，马头琴最早是由察哈尔草原上一个叫苏和的蒙古族牧童做成的。苏和从小由奶奶抚养长大，十七岁时表现出非凡的歌唱天赋。一天，苏和抱回一匹刚出生的白色小马驹，小白马在苏和的精心照管下一天天长大了，美丽又健壮，而且与苏和结下了深厚的情谊。在一年春天的赛马大会上，苏和的白马被王爷看上了。苏和不肯将马卖给王爷，于是王爷下令将苏和打昏，把白马抢走了。几天后的晚上，白马从王府跑了出来，被王府的追兵射中了几箭。它就带着箭跑回了家，死在了苏和的面前。白马的死，给苏和带来了极大的悲伤。一天夜里，苏和在梦里看见白马活了，它轻轻地对他说："你若想让我永远不离开你，，就用我的筋骨做一把琴吧。"苏和醒来以后，就按照小白马的话，用它的骨头、筋和尾做了一把琴。每当他拉起琴来，就会回忆起与白马在一起时的快乐心情，琴声也会变得非常美妙动听。从此，马头琴便成了草原上牧民的传统乐器。

● 马头琴的演奏
Performance of Horsehead Fiddle

Su He and Horsehead Fiddle

Legend has it that the first horsehead fiddle was invented by a Mongol child named Su He on the Chahar grassland. Brought up by his grandmother, Su He showed his phenomenal talent as a singer when he was 17 years old. One day, Su He took in a white newborn pony. Under his tender care, the pony grew up day by day and eventually grew into a strong and beautiful horse in close tie with Su He. One year, in a horse racing convention in the springtime, Su He's white horse was spotted by a duke of the royal families. Since Su He refused to sell the horse to him, the duke ordered his men to knock Su He out of consciousness and took the horse away. At a night several days later, the white horse escaped from the royal family and was chased by the royal family's men. Although shot by several arrows, it managed to arrive home and died in front of Su He. The horse's death brought extreme sadness to Su He. One night in a dream, Su He saw the horse come alive and said to him, "If you want to always keep me by your side, you shall use my sinew and bones to make a fiddle." When he woke up, Su He accordingly used the skull, sinew, and tail of the horse and constructed a fiddle. Whenever he played the fiddle, it would bring back those memories of the happy time when he had been with the white horse, and the music would turn more moving and beautiful. Ever since then, horsehead fiddle has become a comfort for the herdsmen on the grassland.

• 生活在大草原上的蒙古人
The Mongols Living on the Grassland.

艾捷克

艾捷克是起源于古代波斯的一种拉弦乐器，后经"丝绸之路"东传到中国，流行于新疆地区的维吾尔族、乌孜别克族和塔吉克族等少数民族。其外形十分独特，琴筒为球形，木制，内侧蒙蟒皮，通过音柱与桐木板连接，使共鸣体形成两个半球形，周围有发音孔，琴托可转动，用以调整弓与弦的角度。音色具有板面振动与皮面振动相结合的效果。"艾捷克"在维吾尔族语言中是形容开门、关门

• 演奏艾捷克的维吾尔族琴师 <small>（图片提供：CFP）</small>
The Uygur Musician Playing the *Aijieke*

Aijieke

Aijieke is a bowed string instrument originating in ancient Persia and later spread eastward to China through the Silk Road. It is popularized in such ethnic minority groups as the Uyghur, Ozbek, Tajik among others in Xinjiang areas. *Aijieke* has a peculiar outlook with its ball-shaped wood sound box, the inner side of which is covered with python skin. The sound box is connected to the paulownia board through the sound pillar so that the resonator becomes two hemispheres with sound holes surrounding them. The fiddle rest is rotatable for adjusting the angles of the bow and strings. Its timbre combines the vibrations from the board plate as well as the skin plate. The word *Aijieke* in Uygur language refers to the sound made from the act of opening the door, shutting the door, or the spinning of the wagon wheels, to which the sound of this bowed string instrument bears resemblance. And thus *Aijieke* got its name.

The *Aijieke* usually has two major

● 热烈欢快的维吾尔族舞蹈（图片提供：CFP）
The Hot and Joyous Uygur Vocals and Dancing

或车轮轴转动时所发出的声音，与这种拉弦乐器奏出的乐音较为近似，因而得名。

艾捷克一般有两条主奏弦，在主奏弦的弦柱下另设有若干共鸣弦，琴弓用竹片张马尾制成。演奏时，将底柱立于左腿之上或夹于两腿之间，左手持琴按弦，右手持弓摩擦主奏弦，其他弦起共鸣作用。艾捷克因演奏的手法上吸收了提琴、二胡的指法和弓法，可奏出多种美妙的滑音、泛音、和弦和装饰音。

strings. Under the pillars of the major strings are installed several resonance strings. The bow is made of bamboo plate and hairs of horse tails. When played, the base pillar of the instrument is placed either on the left lap or between the legs, with the player's left hand holding the instrument while pressing the strings and the right hand pulling the bow to rub the major strings with resonance from the other supporting strings. Since the performance of *Aijieke* has absorbed the finger skills and bowing techniques from violins and *Er Hu*, it can beautifully produce multiple strains of glides, overtones, chords, and grace notes.

木卡姆

　　木卡姆是流行于中国新疆维吾尔族地区的，以歌、舞、乐综合而成的传统古典大型套曲。15世纪已在新疆各地盛行。歌词多由民间无名歌手所作，也有部分是诗人的作品，内容以爱情为主。现存的木卡姆音乐有多种不同风格的类型，包括喀什木卡姆、多郎木卡姆、哈密木卡姆、吐鲁番木卡姆、伊犁木卡姆等，其中喀什木卡姆形式最完备，更具代表性，而且在天山南北广为流传。喀什木卡姆全部大曲共十二套，又称"十二木卡姆"。

　　十二木卡姆音乐继承和发扬了古代西域音乐的传统，在汉唐时期已形成了完备的艺术形式。16世纪，西域叶尔羌汗国的阿曼尼萨汗王后组织音乐家们将民间流传的十二木卡姆音乐进行了系统的规范，使木卡姆音乐更加完整地保留下来。木卡姆题材多样，节奏错综复杂，曲调极为丰富，以其生动的音乐形象和语言，深沉缓慢的古典叙诵歌曲，热烈欢快的民间舞蹈音乐，流畅优美的叙事组歌，取得了无与伦比的艺术成就。2005年11月，十二木卡姆被联合国教科文组织宣布为"人类口头和非物质遗产代表作"。

● **维吾尔族的木卡姆表演** (图片提供：FOTOE)
Uygur People's Muqam Performance

Muqam

Muqam is a traditional classic great cycles of songs, dance, and music popular in those areas inhabited by the Uygur ethnic group in Xinjiang, where it had already prevailed in the 15th century. The lyrics were mostly written by anonymous singers with a portion done by poets. The contents are centered on love. The existing Muqam music has a great variety in styles including Kashi Muqam, the Dolan Muqam, Kumul Muqam, Turpan Muqam, Yili Muqam and the like, among which Kashi Muqam is a more representative one with the most complete form and widespread in the south and north of Tianshan Mountain. The great cycles of Kashi Muqam has 12 suites, and is also known as "The Twelve Muqams".

The Twelve Muqams have carried on and promoted the tradition of the ancient music in the western regions. They had already had accomplished artistic forms in the Han Dynasty (206 B.C.-220 A.D.) and Tang Dynasty (618-907). In the 16th century, Queen Amannisaham of Yarkant Kingdom in the western regions organized a group of musicians to conduct systematic compilation of the 12 pieces of Muqam music which had been circulating in the local society so that the Muqam music was able to be preserved and passed down. The musical forms of Muqam are diversified in styles with complicated rhythms and rich tunes. Muqam has accomplished incomparable artistic achievements with its lively musical scenes and languages, deep and slow delivery of classical vocals, fervent and fast-paced folk dances, as well as fluent and elegant narrative songs. In November of 2005, the Twelve Muqams were proclaimed by the United Nations Educational, Scientific, and Cultural Organization (UNESCO) as a representative masterpiece of the "Human Oral, and Intangible Cultural Heritage".

传统乐器
Traditional Chinese Musical Instruments

> 弹拨乐器

弹拨乐器是用手指或拨子拨弦，及用琴竹击弦而发音的乐器总称。中国传统弹拨乐器历史悠久，种类形制繁多，大致可以分为三类，一类以长方形琴箱为琴身，平放着弹奏，以古琴为代表；一类包括琴头、琴杆、琴箱几部分，左手按弦，右手弹拨，放在腿上演奏，以琵琶为代表；还有一类就是扬琴，平放而用琴竹击弦取音。

古琴

古琴，又称"瑶琴"，别名"七弦琴"、"玉琴"等，琴身多为狭长的木质音箱，上有厚漆，有七根弦。古琴是世界上最古老的弦乐器之一，也是中国最古老的弹拨乐器，早在春秋时期就已在宫廷

> Plucked String Instrument

The plucked string instrument is a general term for instruments which require the players to use their fingers or plectrums to pluck the strings or use the *Qin Zhu* (a kind of plectrum made of bamboo) to strike the strings to produce sounds. The traditional Chinese plucked string instrument has enjoyed a long history and encompassed a vast variety of shapes which can be generally classified into three different types: the first type is typified by ancient 7-stringed zither with the rectangular body of sound box laid flat to play on; the second type is represented by pear-shaped lute (*Pi Pa*), a plucked string instrument with a fretted fingerboard, composed of such parts as head, pillar, and sound box, and placed on the leg with the left hand pressing the strings and the right hand plucking; the third one is dulcimer (*Yang Qin*), which

和民间流行。据记载，春秋时期的儒家学派创始人孔子就酷爱弹琴，无论在杏坛讲学，还是受困于周游列国的途中，他的琴声始终不绝。

汉代到魏晋南北朝时期，司马相如、蔡邕、嵇康、戴颙等著名文人琴家的出现，对古琴的推广和发展作出了重要的贡献。这一时期，古琴的制作技艺也大有提高，司马相如的"绿绮"琴、蔡邕的"焦

is laid flat for the player to use the *Qin Zhu* to strike the strings for sounds.

Ancient 7-stringed Zither

Ancient 7-stringed zither, also known as *Yao* zither or one of its alias of *Qi Xian* zither or jade zither, has a long and narrow body with a sound box made of wood and painted with lacquer with seven strings. Ancient 7-stringed zither is one of the oldest string instruments in the world and the most ancient plucked

● **清人绘卓文君像**

司马相如是西汉的大文学家、大辞赋家，多才多艺，尤擅操琴。他在临邛的时候，听说大户人家卓王孙的女儿卓文君生得美貌无比，对她非常仰慕。他得知文君正新寡在家，在卓王孙做东的宴席上，为了向卓文君表明心迹，特地抚琴高唱了一首《凤求凰》。躲在门后的卓文君受琴声所感，与司马相如心心相印。当晚，卓文君作出了一个惊世骇俗的决定——与司马相如私奔。"凤求凰"的故事成为人们追求爱情的千古佳话。

Portrait of Zhuo Wenjun by a Painter in the Qing Dynasty (1644-1911)

Sima Xiangru was a leading literary figure and a great master of *Ci Fu* (a sentimental or descriptive composition in ancient China) in the Western Han Dynasty (206 B.C.-25 A.D.) who had multiple gifts, especially playing 7-stringed zither. When he was in Linqiong, he heard Zhuo Wangsun owned a big, rich family and had a very beautiful daughter. He developed a secret crush on her. Learning that Zhuo Wenjun was newly widowed and would attend a banquet hosted by her father, he resorted to the music of 7-stringed zither and performed a song titled *Feng Qiu Huang* (A male phoenix courting his mate). Zhuo Wenjun, who hid behind the door and listened, was greatly moved by the music. On the same evening, she made a shocking decision and eloped with Sima Xiangru. Henceforth, the tale of *Feng Qiu Huang* has become a historic anecdote for people in pursuit of love.

轸池：底板上储放轸子的浅平凹槽。

Tuning Peg Pool: The groove with a flat bottom on the bottom panel to store the tuning pegs.

琴轸：用以调节琴弦松紧长度、改变音高。中心头尾穿通，颈部旁侧有一斜孔与中心孔相通，侧孔斜向顶端。

Tuning Peg: Used to adjust the tension and length of the strings to change the pitch, it is hollow in the center through both ends, with an inclined hole on its neck connecting the hollow center at one end and the other end towards the top.

护轸：底板琴头两侧向下垂凸的部位，保护轸子免受外力碰击。

Tuning Peg Protector: Both corners of head at the bottom pane curved like dog ears to protect tuning pegs from being knocked at.

背面（Back）

龙池、凤沼：琴底部大小两个音槽，位于中部较大的称"龙池"，位于尾部较小的称为"凤沼"，皆为出音孔。

Dragon Pond (*Long Chi*) and Phoenix Swamp (*Feng Zhao*): The two big and small sound grooves at the bottom of the instrument. The big one located in the middle is the dragon pond and the small one at the tail is phoenix swamp. Both are sound holes.

雁足：指龙池与凤沼之间，两只支撑琴体和系缚琴弦的脚，多由坚实木料制成。

Wild Goose Feet (*Yan Zu*): Embedded at the bottom of the instrument and tightly fastened to the bottom panel for the purpose of supporting the body of the instrument and tightening the strings.

承露：岳山边靠头一侧镶嵌的硬木条。

Bearing the Dew (*Cheng Lu*): The hardwood strip by the bridge on the head side.

岳山：额下端镶有架弦的硬木，又称"临岳"，是琴的最高部分。

Bridge (*Yue Shan*): The hardwood part below the forehead, where the string is installed. Also called *Lin Yue* (literally meaning "by the Yue Mountain"), it is the highest point of the instrument.

琴尾：自腰以下称为琴尾。

Zither Tail: The part below the waist.

龙龈：琴尾刻有浅槽用以架弦的硬木。

Dragon Gum (*Long Yin*): The hardwood at the zither tail with shallow grooves to mount the strings.

顶：即琴头上部。

orehead: The upper art of the head.

琴弦：琴面从外向内由粗及细缚弦七根，古时琴弦用蚕丝制成，今多用钢弦。

Strings: Across the front panel from the outer rim to the inner rim are seven strings, lined from the thickest to the thinnest. In ancient times, strings were made of silk, while most of them are now steel.

琴徽：弦外侧的面板上镶嵌的十三个圆点标志，称为徽。为弦的泛音振动节点，在按音弹奏时可作为按音音准的参考。

Badge (*Qin Hui*): On the panel, at the outer side of the strings are marked 13 dots called *Hui*, which represent the pitch points of the overtone vibration and serve as intonation references for finger-pressing during performances.

冠角：龙龈两侧的边饰，又称"焦尾"。

Hat Corner (*Guan Jiao*): The trim on both sides of the dragon gum, also known as burnt tail (*Jiao Wei*).

正面（Front）

• 古琴

Ancient 7-stringed Zither

尾"琴，都是历史上广为传颂的名琴。据说蔡邕在会稽时，听到当地人做饭所烧的木材爆裂的声音，马上辨认出那是一块做琴的良材，赶忙将其从灶中抢出。用这块木材做的琴果然音响极好，但木材尾部已被烧焦，所以名为"焦尾"。

隋唐时期，古琴流传更为广泛，尤其获得文人士大夫的喜爱。当时的王维、李白、白居易、贾岛等许多著名诗人、文人都是古琴的爱好者。在他们的努力下，隋唐时期的古琴出现了新的繁荣景象，涌现出一批影响深远的著名琴家。

宋元以来，古琴的演奏和理论

• 北齐校书图（局部）（北齐）
The Picture of Book Revision Gathering
(Northern Qi Dynasty, 550-577) (Partial)

string instrument in China. It was once popular in both the court and local societies during the Spring and Autumn Period (770 B.C.-476 B.C.). According to records, Confucius, founder of the Chinese philosophy of Confucianism in the Spring and Autumn Period, had a special love for playing the zither. Whether he was teaching at school or stranded halfway in his tour of various states, he would never cease playing the zither and the singing along with it.

The literati musicians from the Han Dynasty (206 B.C.- 220 A.D.) through Wei, Jin, the Southern and Northern Periods (220-589), such as Sima Xiangru, Cai Yong, Ji Kang and Dai Yong, made significant contributions to the promotion and development of ancient 7-stringed zither. During this period, the manufacturing techniques of ancient 7-stringed zither were greatly improved. Sima Xiangru's greenish (*Lü Qi*) zither and Cai Yong's burnt tail (*Jiao Wei*) zither were widely praised zithers in history. It is said Cai Yong was in Kuaiji when he heard the cracking sounds of fire wood that some local people were using to cook food. He recognized it as an excellent material for making a zither and hurriedly saved it from the stove.

传统乐器
Traditional Chinese Musical Instruments

- "鸣凤"琴（宋）

  Ming Feng (phoenix singing) Zither (Song Dynasty 960-1279)

- 王振鹏《伯牙鼓琴图》（元）

  春秋战国时期，楚人俞伯牙和钟子期是一对志同道合的好友，两人一个善弹琴，一个善听琴。伯牙弹琴时志在高山，子期在旁聆听，不由感慨道："善哉，峨峨兮若泰山！"（形容乐曲表现高山气势雄伟之姿）。伯牙继续弹奏，志在流水，子期点头赞叹："善哉！洋洋乎若江河！"（形容乐曲表现江河壮阔之境）。两人心领神会，彼此相通，对于音乐的悟性难分伯仲。伯牙心中所念，俱在琴音中表现出来，而为子期领悟，一曲《高山流水》，缔结了两人喜逢知音的缘分。

  Boya Playing 7-Stringed Zither by Wang Zhenpeng (Yuan Dynasty, 1206-1368)

  In the Spring and Autumn and Warring States Period (770 B.C.-221 B.C.), Yu Boya and Zhong Ziqi were congenial friends in Chu State. Boya was good at playing 7-stringed zither while Ziqi was a good listener. When Boya was playing 7-stringed zither with his mind set on the mountains, Ziqi was listening by his side and exclaimed, "How great it is like the grandeur of the Tai Mountain!" (The music of the 7-strined zither was expressive of the majestic and imposing momentum of the high mountain). Boya continued playing and this time set his mind on the running water while Ziqi nodded his head and proclaimed, "How great it is like the immensity of the rivers!" (The music was expressive of the vast reach of the rivers). The two of them shared tacit comprehension with each other with a comparable understanding of music. What was conceived in Boya's mind was translated into the music played out of his 7-stringed zither and was then intuited by Ziqi. This musical piece *High Mountains and Running Waters* established the predestined bond between the two musical friends.

《听琴图》中的宋徽宗赵佶

这幅画的作者是北宋徽宗赵佶，画中危坐在石墩上作道士打扮的弹琴男子就是徽宗。他微低着头，双手在轻轻拨弄琴弦。

Emperor Hui Zong of Song Dynasty in *Listening to the 7-stringed Zither*

This painting was painted by Zhao Ji, Emperor of Hui Zong of the Northern Song Dynasty (960-1127). The musician in Taoist attire sitting squarely on a stone seat is Hui Zong. He lowered his head, laying both of his hands softly over the 7-stringed zither plucking the strings.

研究都有突出进展，流传到今天的许多琴曲都是在宋代创作完成的名作。宋元时期还出现了不少关于造琴法的专门著作，总结了许多古人造琴工艺的宝贵经验。

为能充分振动，古琴面板一般多用桐木、杉木等松质木料制成。向内外侧呈瓦弧形，与底板胶合而成琴。相传古琴琴身最早是依据凤凰的身形而制，除七根琴弦，还有头、颈、肩、腰、尾、足等部位。琴弦共有七根，传统的琴弦为丝弦。

古琴演奏时通常置于专用的琴桌上，琴额向右，用右手在岳山附近拨弦出声，左手则按弦取音。演

When a zither was finally made out of the wood, it turned out to be as excellent as expected. The pity was that the tail portion of the zither had already been burnt. That is why it was called burnt tail.

In the Sui Dynasty (581-618) and Tang Dynasty (618-907), ancient 7-stringed zither had become even more prevalent and welcomed especially by literati and scholar-bureaucrats. During this period, many prestigious poets like Wang Wei, Li Bai, Bai Juyi, Jia Dao and others were all enthusiasts of ancient 7-stringed zither music. It was under their efforts that a new prosperous phenomenon happened to ancient 7-stringed zither in the Sui Dynasty and

吟徵調高龍下桐
松間疑有入松風
仰窺低審含情客
以聽無絃一弄中
昌永謹題

聽琴圖

Tang Dynasty, and a number of famous and influential ancient 7-stringed zither musicians came into being.

In the Song Dynasty (960-1279) and Yuan Dynasty (1206-1368), the theory and practice of ancient 7-stringed zither experienced breakthroughs in its development. A lot of the musical pieces of ancient 7-stringed zither handed down until today were masterpieces composed in the Song Dynasty. Several books were also released during this period talking about the manufacture of ancient 7-stringed zither and summing up a lot of valuable experiences concerning the making of them since ancient times.

In order to fully vibrate, the front panel of ancient 7-stringed zither is generally made of less solid materials like paulownia, Chinese fir and the like, shaped like a tile arc toward both the inner and the outer sides and conjoined with a base panel. It is said that the body of ancient 7-stringed zither was cast in the form of the body of a phoenix. In addition to the seven strings, it has a head, neck, shoulder, waist, tail and feet.

• 赵佶《听琴图》（北宋）
Listening to the 7-stringed Zither by Zhao Ji (Northern Song Dynasty, 960-1127)

奏者右手的拨弦手指通常留有适度指甲，以利于发音清晰；而左手则不留指甲，便于按弦。古琴的演奏技法复杂而繁多，表现力特别丰富，运用不同的弹奏手法，可以表现出不同的艺术特色。它的高音区清晰明亮、轻松清脆，有如风中铃铎；中音区淳厚纯净、明亮铿锵，犹如敲击玉磬，低音区深沉苍劲、浑厚有力，而丰富的泛音则具有晶莹剔透之感。

The seven strings of ancient 7-stringed zither are traditionally made of silk.

During a performance of an ancient 7-stringed zither, the instrument is usually placed on a special table with the forehead facing to the right for the right hand to pluck the strings around the bridge (*Yue Shan*), while the left hand presses the strings for tune selection. The performer's right finger nails should be kept at a certain length for the sake of crisp sounding effects; the left hand doesn't need long nails for the convenience of pressing strings. The ancient 7-stringed zither has incorporated a great variety of complicated playing skills, expressing rich and mellow sounds. Different applications of skills will produce various artistic flavors. Its treble is bright and clear, as well as relaxed and crisp, like the sounds of wind bells; the mediant is pure and honest and as brilliant as the clanking sounds of jade chimes; in the bass area, its sound is deep and solitarily strong with mature power while the overtone is tainted with a sense of glittering and translucence.

• 黄慎《携琴仕女图》（清）
Picture of a Court Maid Carrying a 7-stringed Zither Drawn by Huang Shen (Qing Dynasty, 1644-1911)

古琴的琴式

　　中国制造古琴的历史极为悠久，制琴名家层出不穷，他们给后世留下了诸多名琴以及各种不同的琴式。古琴有仲尼式、伏羲式、凤势式、连珠式、落霞式、蕉叶式等多种样式，其取名多来自神话传说、历史典故或自然界的物象，每种名称都是一种象征。各种琴式主要是在颈部和腰部向内弯曲上有所不同。

Styles of Ancient 7-stringed Zither

The manufacture of ancient 7-stringed zither has a very long history in China. There have been plenty of zither craftsmen who have left a great number of famous zithers in various styles, such as the Zhong Ni (Confucius) style, Fuxi style, phoenix style, series-wound beads style, sunset cloud style, banana-leaf style, etc. Most of the style names were given from myths and legends, historical anecdotes, or shapes and images in nature. Each name is itself a symbol. Each style differs in the curve on the neck and waist parts of the zither body.

仲尼式

又称"夫子式"，相传为孔子创制，在项腰处各呈方形凹入。

Zhong Ni Style

Also known as Confucius Style, it is said to be invented by Confucius, with rectangular curves on the neck and the waist.

伏羲式

又名"九霄环佩式"，造型宽大古朴，项腰各有一半月形弯入，是最著名的琴式。

Fuxi Style

Also known as jade from heaven style, this is the most noted style of zither, with broad, primitive and unsophisticated flavors; crescent-shaped curves being set in the neck and the waist.

落霞式

在琴的两侧呈对称的波形曲线。

Sunset Cloud Style

Wavy lines were set symmetrically on both sides of the body.

连珠式

为隋逸士李疑所制，项腰各有三个连续半月形弯入，精巧玲珑。

Series-wound Beads Style

Invented by a recluse, Li Yi, in Sui Dynasty (581-618), this style has three consecutive crescent curves on the neck and the waist in a delicate and compact manner.

伏羲造琴的传说

相传天帝伏羲一日巡视至西山桐林时，偶见五星闪烁，霞光万道，天地间的光芒精华尽坠于一棵梧桐树上，正觉得奇怪，忽见两只美丽的大鸟翩然飞至，降落在这棵梧桐树上。这两只鸟一为"凤"，一为"凰"，是罕有的神鸟。伏羲知道凤凰是百鸟之王，对天地间万物异常挑剔，非竹实不食，非梧桐不栖，非醴泉不饮。而今它们单单选择栖息在这棵梧桐树上，可见此梧桐实为树中极品，若用它来造琴，必奏雅乐。当下伏羲便命人将树砍伐，截为三段，将中段梧桐木浸泡在流水中，浸了七十二天之后，选良辰吉日命巧手匠人将其制作成乐器。

伏羲回想百鸟朝凤的情景，据此制定乐曲，供人弹唱。于是每当人间庆贺丰收或遇佳节喜事时，人们便举办盛大的宴会，并在宴会上用新制的乐器弹唱伏羲创造的乐曲，欢喜无限。不久，王母娘娘在天宫瑶池邀请众神，命伏羲将新造的乐器拿来，当场演奏。众天神陶醉在这美妙的音乐中，因见此乐器造型奇特，又是头一回在天宫瑶池见到它，就把它唤作"瑶琴"。

The Legend of Fuxi's Creation of Zither

Legend has it that one day when the Emperor of Heaven Fuxi was on an inspection tour to the paulownia woods in West Mountain, he casually saw five glistening stars shedding myriads of beams together with all the essence of the radiance in the heaven and earth onto one particular paulownia tree. While he was wondering about it, two beautiful giant birds flew in and perched on this paulownia tree. They were a *Feng* bird (male phoenix) and a *Huang* bird (female phoenix), both being the rare spiritual birds. Fuxi knew that *Feng* and Huang were the king and queen of birds and were very particular about everything: they ate nothing but the bamboo fruit, perched on no other trees than paulownia, and drank merely the water in Fountain Li. Now that they chose to perch on this particular paulownia tree, it should be an extremely rare tree among all. If only this tree could be used to construct a zither, it would definitely be capable of delivering the sacred music (*Ya Yue*). He then ordered the tree to be chopped down and cut into three sections. The middle section was submerged in running water for 72 days before it was finally crafted into an instrument by an expertise craftsman ordained on a chosen auspicious date.

Fuxi recalled the scene of hundreds of birds flocking to worship the phoenix, and composed accordingly a musical piece for people to play and sing. As a result, whenever people in the world held celebrations for good harvests or happy holidays, they would host banquets and used the newly manufactured instruments to play and sing the song that Fuxi had made in greatest joys. Before long, the Queen mother of the West invited all the gods to the Yao Pond at the heavenly palace, and Fuxi was also invited to be present with his newly made instrument for performance. All the gods were intoxicated in the beautiful music played out by the instrument. Since this new musical instrument has a peculiar outlook and was debuted in the heaven at the Yao Pond, it was thereafter called Yao zither.

古筝

古筝是一种古老的多弦多柱弹拨乐器，春秋战国时代已流行于秦地（今陕西省西部），故筝自古又被称为"秦筝"，此外，筝还有"银筝"、"云筝"等雅号。对于筝的起源，历史上有许多说法。有种说法认为筝是由另一种弹拨乐器"瑟"演变而来的。传说在很久以前有个人很爱弹瑟，他的两个儿子也都很喜欢瑟，都想把父亲的瑟据为己有。父亲看儿子争执不下，只

Ancient 25-stringed Zither

Ancient 25-stringed zither (*Zheng*) is an ancient plucked string instrument with multiple strings and multiple pillars, which had already been popular in the ancient land of Qin (the western area of present Shaanxi Province) during the Spring and Autumn and Warring States Period (770 B.C.-221 B.C.), and was therefore known also as *Qin Zheng*. In addition to that, it was also elegantly called silver zither, cloud zither, and so on. As for the origin of ancient 25-stringed zither, there have been various versions about it. One of them claimed that ancient 25-stringed zither was a variation from another plucked string instrument "50-stringed zither with moveable bridges *(Se)*". According to the legend, there was once a person who was so into playing 50-stringed zither. His two sons also liked 50-stringed zither and both wanted their father's zither so much. Seeing the sons in contending each other, the father had to cut the 50-stringed zither

- 湖南长沙马王堆汉墓出土的鼓瑟乐俑
The Figurines of Drum and 50-stringed Zither Musicians Unearthed from the Han Dynasty Tomb of *Mawangdui* in Changsha City, Hunan Province

好将50根弦的瑟劈为两半，成为全
新的乐器"筝"。

古筝的外形近似于长箱，一般
由红木制成，主要由面板、底板、
边板组成，面板中间稍微凸起，底
板呈平面或近似于平面。筝弦张在
面板上，一般用丝弦或钢丝弦。每
根弦都由一个"雁柱"支撑在面板
上，雁柱可以自由移动，以调节音
高。最早的筝以二十五弦最多，唐
宋时有十三弦筝，后增至十六根、
十八弦、二十一弦等，目前最常用
的规格为二十一弦，按五声音阶排
列定弦。

古筝的演奏手法非常丰富，可
以用双手一起弹奏旋律，也可以用

into halves, and that was the beginning of
the new instrument 25-stringed zither.

Looking like a long box, ancient
25-stringed zither is generally made of
redwood and composed of the front panel,
the bottom panel, and the side boards.
The center of the front panel bulges out
a little bit, and the bottom panel is flat
or nearly flat. The strings spreading over
the front panel are usually silk or steel
strings, each of which is supported by a
wild goose pillar (Yan Zhu) on the panel.
The wild goose pillar is flexibly movable
to adjust the pitch sound. At first, this
instrument had 25 strings. In the Tang
Dynasty (618-907) and Song Dynasty
(960-1279), it had only 13 strings and
the number was later increased to 16,

• 古筝
Ancient 25-stringed Zither

右手弹奏，左手按雁柱左侧的弦，以产生滑音等效果。筝的音色清亮、圆润、纯净、柔美，旋律抑扬顿挫、华丽流畅，非常动听，既可独奏，亦适于伴唱。

18, 21, and so forth. Currently it has the specification of 21 strings arranged in fixed way according to the pentatonic scale.

Ancient 25-stringed zither has a very rich variety of manual playing skills. It can be played by both hands, or by the right hand while the left hand presses the strings on the left side of the Yan Zhu in order to produce effects such as glides. The timbre of 25-stringed zither sounds clear and bright, full and mellow, pure and soft, set in the rise and fall of beautiful rhythms with fluency and elegance. It can be played solo or accompanies with vocals.

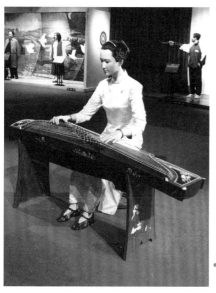

• 古筝的演奏
Performance of Ancient 25-stringed Zither

吕布鼓筝逃一劫

吕布是三国时期一位骁勇善战的武将。他曾经帮助袁绍攻打拥兵数万的张燕，战功显赫。可事后论功行赏时，吕布却遭到袁绍其他部将的妒忌和排挤，他心生不满。这时有人便向袁绍献计说："吕布迟早会离开，放走他等于放虎归山，不如趁他现在羽翼未丰除掉他。"袁绍点头称是，暗中部署。不久，吕布果然向袁绍提出要离开。当天晚上，三十多名手持利器的武士将吕布的营帐团团包围。突然，军帐里传出了喧闹之声，原来是吕布在和众军士饮酒道别。而喧笑声中还夹杂着一缕筝声。乐声忽而清亮，忽而轻柔，忽而低回，忽而圆润，美妙绝伦，令人陶醉其中不能自拔。帐外的将士听得入迷，不知不觉间天快大亮了，他们这才想起身负刺杀吕布的重任，连忙拔出刀剑冲了进去。然而出人意料的是，营帐中只有一名歌伎正披着吕布的斗篷在弹筝，哪里还有吕布的身影？

武士们大惊失色，逼问歌伎才知道，吕布察觉了袁绍的阴谋，请来一些客人饮酒听琴，并亲自鼓筝助兴。当客人们陆续走出帐篷时，吕布便混在其中。当时守候在外的武士们听得太过入迷，没有仔细察看这些客人的形貌。就这样，吕布凭借鼓筝巧妙逃过一劫。

Lü Bu Made an Escape by Playing 25-stringed Zither

Lü Bu was a valiant and belligerent martial general in Three Kingdom Period (220-280). He had helped Yuan Shao against Zhang Yan's tens of thousands of soldiers with remarkable achievements in battle fields. But when it came to the time of rewarding in accordance with the merits, he was envied and elbowed out by the other generals, which set him in a very unsatisfactory mindset. It was right at this point that someone offered Yuan Shao a suggestion and said, "It's a matter of sooner or later for Lü Bu to take leave and it will be just like setting free a tiger back to the wild. It would be better to take his life before it is too late." Yuan Shao nodded in agreement and ordered the plan to be secretly prepared. Before long, Lü Bu did ask for leave. On the very night, 30 appointed warriors with sharp weapons surrounded Lü Bu's camp when they suddenly heard a fit of noises coming out of the camp. It was Lü Bu holding a farewell party with his soldiers and men inside the camp. In the midst of the noise was a strain of music from 25-stringed zither going out loud and bright, and then soft and light, and at the next moment full and mellow. The instrument was so wonderfully played and fascinating that the warriors outside the camp were carried away before they finally realized it's nearly dawn and had to execute the task of assassinating Lü Bu. They drew out their blades and swords and charged into the camp. To their surprise, they only found a female singer in Lü Bu's cape playing the 25-stringed zither. Lü Bu was nowhere to be found.

The warriors were quite frightened, and questioned the singer about what had happened. They were told that after perceiving Yuan Shao's scheme, Lü Bu invited a group of guests to drink and listen to the zither performance. Lü Bu personally performed the 25-stringed zither to add to the fun. When the guests left one after another, Lü Bu hid himself among them. The warriors had been so enchanted by the music that they missed out on recognizing Lü's face among the retreating guests. So, Lü Bu had successfully got away thanks to the ancient 25-stringed zither performance.

琵琶

　　琵琶是一种历史悠久的弹拨乐器，最早起源于东亚地区，由印度经西域传入中国内地。早期的琵琶具有梨形音箱、曲颈、四柱、四弦，用拨片演奏，被称为"批把"，汉代刘熙《释名·释乐器》中解释道：批把来自西域胡人，是

Pear-shaped Lute

Pear-shaped lute (*Pi Pa*) is a plucked string instrument with a long historic background. Originating in the areas of Eastern Asia, it was introduced into China from India through the western regions. The early pear-shaped lute had pear-shaped sound box, curved neck, four columns and four strings, and was played with a plectrum. It was called *Pi Ba*. As stated in *Shi Ming* (Explanation of Names): *Explanation of Musical Instruments* by Liu Xi of the Han Dynasty (206 B.C.- 220 A.D.), Pi Ba came from the uncivilized people of the western regions, and was played while riding on the horseback. While playing it, the action of plucking forward is called *Pi*, and the action of plucking backward is called *Ba*. By the Wei and Jin Period (220-420), *Pi Ba* was officially named *Pi Pa*. During the Sui Dynasty (581-618) and Tang Dynasty (618-907), pear-

• 弹琵琶者砖雕（五代）
  Brick Sculpture of Pear-shaped Lute Player (Five Dynasties, 907-960)

白釉陶弹琵琶女佣（隋）
White Glazed Ceramic of the
Pear-shaped-Lute-playing Maid
(Sui Dynasty, 581-618)

骑在马上弹奏的乐器，向前弹出称"批"，向后挑进称"把"。到了魏晋时期，批把正式定名为"琵琶"。隋唐时期，琵琶已成为燕乐歌舞的主要乐器，从敦煌壁画和云冈石窟壁画中，仍能见到它在当时乐队中的地位。唐代后期，琵琶从演奏技法到制作构造上都得到了很大的发展，在演奏上最突出的变化是由横抱演奏变为竖抱演奏，而且用手指直接弹奏取代了用拨片弹奏发声。

宋元明清时期，琵琶的性质已逐步稳定，而且从宋末开始出现了琵琶的大型套曲结构形式。明清时期，琵琶在民间更是大为发展，在各种歌舞、戏曲、曲艺中得到广泛的应用。

shaped lute had become an essential instrument in *Yan* music and dances. Its status among the band of the time can still be seen in the murals of Dunhuang and Yungang Grottoes.

In the late Tang Dynasty, pear-shaped lute had witnessed great development and progress in the playing skills as well as the manufacturing structures. The most prominent change in the playing style was the transition from the horizontal way of holding it to the vertical one as well as the plectrum being replaced by fingers directly.

In Song Dynasty (960-1279), Yuan Dynasty (1206-1368), Ming Dynasty (1368-1644) and Qing Dynasty (1644-1911), the nature of pear-shaped lute gradually stabilized, with large-scale suites of composition being developed toward the end of the Song

琴头：琵琶的最上部分，用于装饰和固定弦轴，大多做成"玉如意"形状。

Head: The uppermost portion of the pear-shaped lute. It is used as a decoration and to secure the pegs. It is commonly in the shape of Jade *Ru Yi* (*Ru Yi* is a curved decorative object symbolizing power and good fortune in Chinese folklore).

相位：又称"颈"部，呈三角形的菱柱体，共有六个，是一种音位装置，一般由木材、牛角、骨头制成。

Xiang Wei: The six triangular prisms at the upper "neck" part of pear-shaped lute serving as a type of phonological device. It is commonly made of wood, ox horns, or bones.

山口：琴身和琴头连接处的四个弦槽，用于搁弦。

Shan Kou: the four grooves for the strings located at the connection part of body and head. It is used to mount the strings.

品位：位于面板上的竹条，共有二十四个，同相位一起构成了音域宽广的十二平均律。

Frets: A total of 24 bamboo strips located on the main ban，together with the Xiang Wei, they form the broad diapason of 12 equal temperament.

弦：由尼龙线或高级钢丝缠制而成。

Strings: Made of twisted nylon lines or high-class steel wires

覆手：在面板的下半部分，具有系弦和传振的作用。四条弦系在覆手的四个小孔内。

Fu Shou: Located at the bottom portion of the front panel, it is used to secure the strings and transmit vibrations. The four strings are tied within the four small holes located in the Fu Shou.

面板：镶嵌于琴身上的共鸣板，上狭下阔，底呈半圆，中空，材料一般选用桐木。

Front Panel: It is embedded on the resonator board of body, narrow at the top and wide at the bottom in semi-circular shape and hollowed in the center. Front panel is commonly made of paulownia wood.

琴身：琵琶的最大组成部分，通常由整块木料挖成半瓢形状，和面板粘接在一起构成共鸣箱体。

Body: As the largest part of pear-shaped lute, it is commonly shaped by carving a half gourd shape from an entire piece of wood, and bonded together with the front panel to form the resonator box.

琵琶
Pear-shaped Lute

琵琶演奏技巧复杂繁多，可演奏多种和音、和弦。琵琶发出的基音中又伴有丰富的泛音，穿透力强，高音区明亮而富有刚性，中音区柔和而有润音，低音区音质淳厚。

Dynasty. During the Qing Dynasty and Ming Dynasty, the pear-shaped lute saw significant development in folk societies, and was widely used in various dances, operas and folk performances.

The playing skills of pear-shaped lute vary in complexity, and can be used to play an array of accords and chords. The keynote of the pear-shaped lute is accompanied by rich overtones with strong penetrating power; its high-pitched area is bright and stiff, mediant area sounds gentle and smooth, and bass area encompasses pure yet profound sounds.

• 吴伟《琵琶美人图》（明）
Picture of Pear-shaped-Lute-playing Beauty by Wu Wei (Ming Dynasty, 1368-1644)

千古绝唱《琵琶行》

　　唐代元和十一年（816年）深秋的一天，浔阳江边（今江西省九江市境内）秋风瑟瑟，荻花丛中隐约传出美妙的琵琶声。正在江头与客送别的江州司马白居易蓦闻此声，不由出神。只见一艘小船缓缓驶了过来，白居易忙邀船中人移船相见，原来弹琵琶的是一位容貌姣好的女子，她接受了白居易的邀请。

　　席间，白居易询问琵琶女的身世，原来她是长安的歌伎，自幼师从名家学习琵琶，不知有多少名人倾倒于她的风采。而风月场中的欢乐转瞬即逝。虽然她后来嫁给了一个商人，但是聚少离多，她也唯有独守着空船，轻弹一曲诉诉心中之事。白居易听完琵琶女的故事，不由长叹：这身世飘零的琵琶女与自己何其相似啊。自己也曾才高位显身居京城，而今却因直言而遭贬斥，来到这荒凉之地。他不由得发出了"同是天涯沦落人，相逢何必曾相识"的感慨。白居易整装起身，恳请她再弹一曲，而他也和着琴声，创作了一首长诗《琵琶行》："……大弦嘈嘈如急雨，小弦切切如私语。嘈嘈切切错杂弹，大珠小珠落玉盘……"琵琶动人的音调，琵琶女高超的演技，琵琶的弦外之音，一份古今相通的身世之感，让人们千载之下，恍如身临其境。

The Masterpiece of *Song of Pear-shaped Lute*

On a late autumn day in the 11th year of the Yuanhe Period (816) in Tang Dynasty, as the autumn wind whistled by the Xunyang River (in the area of Jiujiang City, Jiangxi Province), the faint yet wonderful sound of pear-shaped lute could be heard from behind the bushes of silver-grass flowers. Bai Juyi, Sima (an official title) of Jiangzhou, who was bidding farewell to his guests by the river, couldn't help but lose his thoughts in the music. As a boat slowly drew closer, Bai quickly went to welcome the boat and requested to meet the person in it. It turned out that the one who was playing the pear-shaped lute was a beautiful woman in the boat, and she accepted Bai's invitation.

　　During the meeting, Bai enquired the pear-shaped lute-playing woman about her background. She was actually a female singer from Chang' an City, who had studied the pear-shaped lute under a famous teacher since childhood. There had been numerous famous people being overwhelmed by her presence. However, the joys of the pleasure quarter were but too brief. Although later she had married a merchant, they were more living apart than staying together. Therefore, she was holding onto the empty boat alone, and confided her feelings to the playing of pear-shaped lute. After hearing to the woman's story, Bai could not help but draw a long sigh: The life of this wandering woman with the pear-shaped lute was so similar to his own. He himself was once holding a high-ranked position in the capital, but was later denounced for speaking too straightforward, and exiled to this desolate place. He could not help but feel that "for those people suffering the same misfortune,

传统乐器
Traditional Chinese Musical Instruments

there is no need for them to know each other before they meet." Bai stood up and composed himself, then requested her to play one more song. Along with the song, Bai composed a long poem *Song of Pear-shaped Lute*: "...large strings giving pounding sounds like the rain, while small strings murmuring earnestly. With the pounding and murmuring played in a mixed manner, it sounds like large and small beads of pearls falling into a jade plate...." This tale of the moving tone of the pear-shaped lute, the superb performance from the woman, the overtone of the pear-shaped lute, and a sense of life experiences transcending the boundary of the past and the present make people feel as if they were still in the original scene even after thousands of years.

● 郭诩《琵琶行图轴》（明）
Scroll Painting of Song of Pear-shaped Lute
by Guo Xu (Ming Dynasty, 1368-1644)

箜篌

箜篌是十分古老的弹弦乐器，两千多年前就已出现，最初称"坎侯"或"空侯"，在古代除宫廷雅乐使用外，在民间也广泛流传。盛唐时期，随着经济文化的飞速发展，箜篌演奏也达到了相当高的水平，也就是在这个时期，中国古代的箜篌先后传入日本、朝鲜等邻国。在日本奈良东大寺的寺院中，至今还保存着两架唐代箜篌残品。但是，这种古老的乐器从14世纪后期便不再流行，以致慢慢消失了，人们现在只能在古代壁画和浮雕上看到一些箜篌的图样。

中国古代有卧箜篌、竖箜篌、凤首箜篌三种形制。竖箜篌的来源

Chinese Harp

Chinese harp (*Kong Hou*), originally named *Kan Hou or Kong Hou,* is a very ancient plucked string instrument that appeared as early as two thousand years ago. In addition to being used for the court music *Ya* music in the ancient palace, it was also widely circulated in local societies. During the flourishing Tang Dynasty, as the economy and culture rapidly developed, the performance of Chinese harp had also reached a very high level. It was also during this period that the ancient Chinese harp was introduced into Japan, Korea and other neighboring countries successively. Two old Chinese harps from the Tang Dynasty are still preserved to this day in the Todaiji Temple located in Nara, Japan. Somehow, this ancient musical instrument was no longer popular in late 14th century, and was slowly disappeared. Nowadays, people can only see pictures of Chinese harp on ancient murals and relief sculptures.

• 彩绘陶弹箜篌女乐俑（隋）
Colored Ceramic of Female Musicians Playing Chinese Harp (Sui Dynasty, 581-618)

可以追溯到古代西方十分流行的一种叫做"竖琴"的乐器。在汉魏壁画上可见到弹奏竖箜篌的人像，画中的箜篌与亚述浮雕上的竖琴十分相近。竖箜篌状如半截弓背，曲形的共鸣槽设在向上弯曲的曲木上，

• 弹箜篌者砖雕（五代）
Brick Sculpture of a Chinese Harp Player (Five Dynasties, 907-960)

There were three different types of Chinese harp in ancient China: lying-down Chinese harp, vertical Chinese harp, and phoenix-head Chinese harp. The vertical Chinese harp can be traced back to the harp popular in the ancient western world. On the murals of the Han Dynasty (206 B.C.-220 A.D.) and Wei Dynasty (220-265) where images of people playing vertical Chinese harp can be spotted, the depicted instruments look very much like those harps in the relief sculptures of Assyria. The vertical Chinese harp looks like a half of a bow with the curved resonator groove set in the curved wood tilting upwards, coupled with pillar stand and stall bars as well as more than 20 strings. The player is supposed to hold the Chinese harp vertically in the chest and use the thumbs and index fingers of both hands to play on the strings. For this reason, playing Chinese harp was also called by people in the Tang Dynasty (618-907) as "upholding Chinese harp". The phoenix-head Chinese harp is pretty similar in forms to the vertical Chinese harp, with the sound box set in the cross wood-piece at the bottom in the shape of a boat, and the upward curved wood either containing pegs or functioning as pegs to

并有脚柱和肋木，张有20多条弦。演奏者要将箜篌竖抱于怀，从两面用双手的拇指和食指同时弹奏，因此唐代人又称演奏箜篌为"擎箜篌"。凤首箜篌形制与竖箜篌相近，其音箱设在下方横木的部位，呈船形，向上的曲木则设有轸或起轸的作用，用以紧弦。曲颈项端雕有凤头。

卧箜篌最早出现在春秋时的楚国，与琴、瑟十分相似，最大的不同是其长形共鸣体音箱的面板上有像琵琶一样的品位。汉代箜篌十分流行，汉乐府诗《孔雀东南飞》中，即有"十五弹箜篌，十六诵诗书"的

● **舞乐图（局部）（唐）**
这是六扇绢制屏风中的一扇，上绘一位乐伎怀抱卧箜篌，头戴绣花帽，足蹬皮靴，面颊丰腴。

Picture of Musical Dance (partial) (Tang Dynasty, 618-907)
This is one of the six silk-made serial screens painted with a musician of chubby cheeks, holding a lying-down Chinese harp, in an embroidered hat and a pair of high-heeled boots.

adjust the tension of the strings. The top of the curved neck is sculptured as a phoenix head.

The lying-down Chinese harp first appeared in the state of Chu during the Spring and Autumn Period (770 B.C.-476 B.C.), and looked similar to 7-stringed zither and 50-stringed zither with the biggest difference in the frets, like those in pear-shaped lute, set on the front panel of the rectangular resonator box. The lying-down Chinese harp was very popular in the Han Dynasty (206 B.C.- 220 A.D.). In the *Yue Fu* poem *The Peacock Flies to the Southeast* of Han Dynasty, there's such a line saying that "playing Chinese harp at fifteen and reciting *The Book of Songs* and *The Book of History* at sixteen." After Song Dynasty (960-1279),

诗句。宋代以后卧箜篌在中国日渐消亡，但在朝鲜却得以传承，经过历代的改进成为今日的玄琴。

the lying-down Chinese harp gradually slipped into disappearance in China but was carried on in ancient Korea and improved through generations in the present form of geomungo.

《箜篌引》

《箜篌引》又名《公无渡河》，是一首汉代古诗。据记载，在汉代一天早晨，黄河边一位撑船摆渡的船夫望见一个披散白发、疯疯癫癫的人提着酒壶朝着河岸奔走，眼看就要冲进急流之中了。他的妻子追在后面大声呼喊着，让他不要渡河，却已赶不及了，那个疯子冲进了河里，被白浪吞没了。那位女子悲痛之下，拨弹箜篌，唱了起来："公无渡河，公竟渡河！堕河而死，将奈公何！"其声凄怆万分，一曲唱罢，她也投河而死。船夫回到家，把这件事和那妇人的歌向妻子作了描绘，妻子听后也甚为悲伤，于是弹着箜篌把歌记录下来。后来听到这首歌的人无不落泪。这就是《箜篌引》这首诗歌的来历。全诗虽只有短短四句十六个字，由于情真意切，深受历代诗人的喜爱。唐代大诗人李白、李贺、温庭筠、王建等人都曾以同样的题目和素材进行过再次创作。

Song of Chinese Harp

Song of Chinese Harp, also known as *Don't Cross the River, Sir*, was an ancient poem in the Han Dynasty (206 B.C.- 220 A.D.). It describes the tale that one morning in Han Dynasty, a ferryman working at the bank of the Yellow River saw a man with unbound white hair running crazily to the bank with a bottle of alcohol and was on the verge of dashing into the torrents. His wife was running after him and yelled to stop him from plunging into the river. However, it was too late, for the mad man was already in the middle of the river and swallowed by the high tides. Breaking into grief, the wife took out her Chinese harp and sang "Don't cross the river, sir! You simply ran into the river. Since you are drowned in the river, what should I do?" The song was so sad and desperate. After the singing, the wife plunged herself into the river too and perished. After returning home, the ferryman told his wife about what had happened and the song. Hearing that, the saddened wife took out her Chinese harp and replayed the song. Later, whoever heard the song would be moved to tears. This is the origin of the *Song of Chinese Harp*. The whole poem has only four lines and 16 Chinese characters. Due to its truthfulness and sincerity, the poem has been favored by many poets through generations. Such great Tang Dynasty (618-907) poets as Li Bai, Li He, Wen Tingyun, Wang Jian, and others had re-written the poem with the same title and the same materials.

忽雷

　　忽雷是一种产生于唐代的弹拨乐器，形制与琵琶十分相似。"忽雷"这个名称的来历，有许多不同的说法。有人认为，"忽雷"一词在古代原指鳄鱼，用其牙齿做乐器称为"忽雷"。还有人认为，"忽雷"是因其发音"忽忽若雷"而得名。

　　忽雷音色清越且具有较强的穿透力，是古代巧匠智慧的结晶。它从宫廷散落民间，在千年间流传，又经历代文人的诗文渲染，其价值早已超越一般的古乐器，可谓是古代乐器文化与历史发展的见证。

Hu Lei

Originating in Tang Dynasty (618-907), *Hu Lei* is a plucked string instrument very similar to pear-shaped lute in shape. There have been different versions as to the origin of its name *Hu Lei*. Some people thought that the term *Hu Lei* was the ancient name for crocodiles. Since the instrument was made of the animal's teeth, it was thus named accordingly. Other people held the idea that it was named because the music it produced sounded like the thunders.

Hu Lei does have a clear and powerful penetrating sound. It's a result of wisdom from ancient craftsmen. It was brought to the local societies from the court and has undergone so many times of changes in the major players in a matter of some thousand years. With the promotion and propaganda from the literati in different ages, the value of *Hu Lei* has already exceeded the ordinary ancient instruments, and it certainly deserves being called the witness of the cultural and historical development of ancient musical instruments.

中国乐器大家族　The Extended Family of Chinese Musical Instruments

● 大忽雷
Big *Hu Lei*

小忽雷的传奇

唐代德宗年间（780—805），当朝宰相是著名的画家韩滉。一次，他在四川得到一块珍贵的紫檀木，请工匠参考琵琶的形状创制了两件弦乐器，一大一小，分别称为"大忽雷"和"小忽雷"，进献给皇帝。

唐大和九年（835年），宫廷发生"甘露之变"，唐武宗李炎继位，小忽雷在宫乱中不知流落何方。到了清代，著名戏曲家孔尚任于1698年在北京得到了小忽雷，十分欣喜，把小忽雷的故事编成戏剧《小忽雷》。后来，小忽雷辗转流传不知所往，到了20世纪初，一位名叫刘世珩的人刊印孔尚任的《小忽雷》，引起人们的注意，收藏小忽雷的收藏家就把这珍贵的琴送给了他。为此，他特地建了"小忽雷阁"，还邀请乐师到阁中弹奏小忽雷。事有凑巧，在"小忽雷阁"听琴的人中，有个叫张瑞山的人藏有一把二弦琵琶，取来一看，正是大忽雷。于是，张瑞山把大忽雷也送给了刘世珩。刘世珩把"小忽雷阁"改名为"双忽雷阁"，又收集了所有关于大小忽雷的记载，编辑成书。

清末到民国时期，在军阀混战之中，小忽雷再度消失，直到上世纪50年代初国家文物局才再次寻访到小忽雷，交由故宫博物院保存。如今藏于故宫博物院的琴颈正面的山口下方，刻有篆书银嵌"小忽雷"三字，背面刻有"臣滉手制恭献建中辛酉春"楷书十一字，可知正是当时韩滉所制的小忽雷。故宫博物院还藏有大忽雷，形状与小忽雷相似，以蟒皮蒙腹，也张两根弦，据考证是清代仿造。

The Legend of the Small *Hu Lei*

In the reign of Emperor Dezong (780-805) in the Tang Dynasty, when Han Huang, a well-known painter, served as the prime minister, he came across a very valuable rosewood block in Sichuan Province. He hired the craftsman to construct two string musical instruments out of the block in imitation of the shape of pear-shaped lute. The big one was called big *Hu Lei* and the small one was called small *Hu Lei*. Both were presented to the Emperor as gifts.

In the 9th year of Dahe Period (835) in Tang Dynasty, when the Ganlu Incident in the court had pushed Li Yan to the throne as Emperor Wuzong, the small *Hu Lei* was missing during the incident. In Qing Dynasty (1644-1911), the well-known dramatist, Kong Shangren, unexpectedly discovered the small *Hu Lei* in 1698 in Beijing. He joyfully wrote the story in a play called *Small Hu Lei*. Later, the small *Hu Lei* had passed through many hands and many places until it was missing again. In the beginning of the 20th century, a man named Liu Shiheng re-published Kong's *Small Hu Lei* and aroused people's attention. The person who had collected the small Hu Lei thus gave this valuable instrument to Liu as a gift. For this, Liu built a pavilion named Small *Hu Lei* Pavilion and invited musicians there to play the small *Hu Lei*. It happened so coincidentally that among the audience at the Small *Hu Lei* Pavilion, a man called Zhang Ruishan had collected a two-string pear-shaped lute.

It turned out to be the big *Hu Lei*. After Zhang gave the big *Hu Lei* to Liu as a gift, Liu changed the name of the pavilion into Double *Hu Lei* Pavilion and then collected all the records and literature about the big and small *Hu Lei* and compiled them into a volume.

From the end of the Qing Dynasty (1644-1911) to the Republican Period (1912-1949), the small *Hu Lei* disappeared again in the confusion of the tangled warfare among warlords. It was at the beginning of the 50s in last century that the State Administration of Cultural Heritage searched and rediscovered the small *Hu Lei* and handed it to the custody of the Palace Museum. On the instrument which is now preserved in the Palace Museum, there are three silver-colored Chinese characters *Xiao Hu Lei* (small *Hu Lei*) in seal scripts right below the *Shan Kou* at the front side of the neck. On the back are carved the eleven characters in regular script: "Personally manufactured by official Huang and sincerely presented in the Spring of Xinyou year during the reign of Jianzhong." This is obviously the small *Hu Lei* that was made by Han Huang. Also preserved in the Palace Museum is a big *Hu Lei* in similar shape to the small *Hu Lei*, with the belly covered with python skin and two strings as well. According to the verification, it was an imitation instrument made in Qing Dynasty.

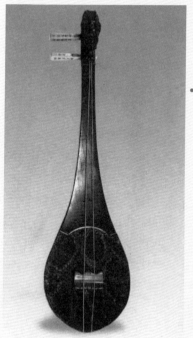

小忽雷

小忽雷琴身全长45厘米，腹宽16厘米，由整块硬木制作而成。琴的下部雕凿出椭圆形的腹腔，其上蒙以蟒皮，形成半梨形的共鸣箱。琴的上部为上窄下宽的琴颈，不设品位，正下方开有一个扁长形的出音孔，琴头雕刻着极为精致的龙头，龙口里还含着一粒活动的小圆珠。琴头曲项的左侧，装有两个用象牙制作的琴轸。

Small *Hu Lei*

The small *Hu Lei*, 45 cm long in total and 16 cm wide in the belly, is made of a whole block of hardwood. The bottom of the instrument was carved hollow in an oval shape and covered with the python skin, which forms the resonator box in a shape of a half pear. The upper part is the neck, narrow at the top and wide at the bottom with no frets on it. Directly below the neck is a narrow rectangular sound hole. The head is carved exquisitely into a dragon head, whose mouth holds a small movable ball. On the left side of the curved neck at the head are installed two pegs made of ivory.

柳琴

柳琴原是流行于山东、安徽、江苏一带的民间乐器，它可用来弹奏简单歌曲，也可以给柳琴戏、泗州戏等地方戏曲做伴奏。其发音铿锵有力，音色高昂激越。柳琴又因其外形质朴，民间气息浓厚，而被百姓称为"土琵琶"。

最早的柳琴构造较简单，只有两条丝弦，七个用高粱秆做成的品位，音域很窄，还不便转调。当时的琴体较大，演奏时有一竹筒套在

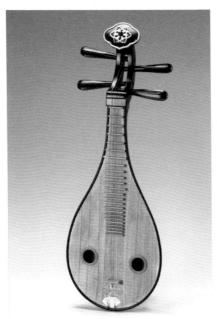

● 柳琴（图片提供：全景正片）
Liu Qin

Liu Qin

Liu Qin is a local instrument popular in Shandong, Anhui, and Jiangsu provinces, and applied in the accompanying music of such folk operas as *Liu Qin* opera, Sizhou opera, and the like, or in simple performance of songs. It has loud and sonorous volume as well as high-pitched and sturdy timbre. Due to its rustic outlook with dense folk flavors, it is intimately known by local people as the rustic pear-shaped lute (*Tu Pi Pa*).

The earliest *Liu Qin* had a very simple structure with only two strings and seven frets made of sorghum stems. Its narrow diapason doesn't allow for modulation. In the beginning, the body of *Liu Qin* was quite massive, and it was performed in a stylish way because it needed the player to wear a bamboo tube on the index finger and pinch it tight with the thumb, while whipping the wrist to pluck the strings for sounding. As the development progressed, it has gradually become a solo performance instrument and is usually the high-pitched instrument in the band of ethnic music. It has a special sound effect, which is not easily covered by other instruments, so it

食指上，用拇指捏紧，靠手腕甩动而拨弦发音，演奏形式独具特色。经过长时间的发展，现已成为独奏乐器，并常用于民族乐队中的高音乐器，音响效果独特，不易被其他乐器所掩盖，常用来演奏高音区的主旋律，有时也演奏华丽、技巧性高的华彩乐段。它既适于演奏活泼欢快、对比强烈、节奏鲜明的曲调，也适于表现优美抒情的旋律，在乐队中能与琵琶、阮、筝和二胡等乐器和谐地合奏。

阮

阮是一种弹拨乐器，在古代又被叫做"秦琵琶"。

在西晋时期，有一位叫阮咸的音乐家，非常善于弹奏这种有圆形音箱的"秦琵琶"，由于他的演奏技艺高超，深受人们的喜爱，人们就渐渐用他的名字"阮咸"来称呼这种乐器了。到了宋代，阮咸被简称为"阮"。

is often used to play the theme in high-pitched area. Occasionally, it is used to play a featured section of splendid music with highlighted skills. On the one hand, it fits for the performance of lively, fast-paced, high-contrast tunes with clear beats, and on the other hand, it is also capable of expressing graceful and lyric melodies. In the band, it harmoniously blends into the ensemble with pear-shaped lute, moon-shaped lute, 25-stringed zither, *Er Hu* and the others.

Moon-shaped Lute

Moon-shaped lute (*Ruan*) is a plucked string instrument and was also called Qin pear-shaped lute in ancient times.

In the Western Jin Period (265-316), a musician called *Ruan Xian* was very good at playing this Qin pear-shaped lute, which had a round sound box. Due to his

● 河北赵州柏林禅寺持阮飞天像
Picture of Flying Apsaras with Moon-shaped Lute in Bolin Zen Monastery in Zhaozhou, Hebei Province

• 阮（图片提供：全景正片）
Moon-shaped Lute

excellent playing skills, he was so widely favored by people that they began to call this instrument by his name *Ruan Xian*. In the Song Dynasty (960-1279), *Ruan Xian* was further shortened into Ruan.

The outlook of moon-shaped lute is quite simple with three parts: head, pillar, and body. The head is usually decorated with the Chinese traditional artifacts of bone sculpture in the form of dragon, *Ru Yi*, and others, with four pegs on both sides. The body of moon-shaped lute is an oblate resonator box composed of the glued parts of front panel, the back panel, and the frame board. Moon-shaped lute shares the same structural principle and construction materials with pear-shaped lute. Moon-shaped lute is played in a very similar way to pear-shaped lute, having the left hand press on the strings and the thumb and index finger of the right hand stalled for plucking. However, its playing skills are simpler than pear-shaped lute's, moon-shaped lute is characterized by its full and mellow sound and has irreplaceable effects in the musical band.

　　阮的外形很简单，由琴头、琴杆和琴身三个部分组成。琴头一般装饰有中国传统的龙或如意等骨雕艺术品，两侧装有四个弦轴。阮的琴身是一个扁圆形的共鸣箱，由面板、背板和框板胶合而成。阮的结构原理、制作材料和琵琶都有很多相同之处。其演奏姿式也和琵琶相近，左手按琴弦，右手拇指、食指带指套弹奏，而演奏技巧比琵琶简单。阮音色圆润而丰厚，颇具特色，在乐队中起到不可替代的作用。

• 仇英《停琴听阮图》（明）

在深山幽涧旁，两位高士奏乐，弹琴者停下手来，静听弹阮者演奏，两人神清气爽，在高山流水旁弹奏清音，整个画面色彩淡雅，清澈灵动。

Stop the 7-stringed Zither to Hear Moon-shaped Lute by Qiu Ying (Ming Dynasty, 1368-1644)

By a hidden stream in the depth of a mountain, two people were performing music. The one playing the 7-stringed zither stopped to listen to the moon-shaped lute played by the other. Both looked bright and spirited with clear music played by the running water within a high mountain. The entire scene is in light and elegant colors with lucent and vigorous flavors.

与猪共饮的阮咸

阮咸，字仲容，陈留尉氏（今河南省开封市附近）人。与嵇康、阮籍、山涛、向秀、刘伶、王戎并称"竹林七贤"。他不仅精通音律，而且生性放浪不羁，留下了许多为人称道的趣闻轶事。一次，阮咸去参加阮氏宗族的聚会，席间大家高兴起来，提议不再用平常的小杯子喝酒，而改用大瓮盛酒。众人围坐在酒瓮边，相对畅饮。正在这时，院中的一群猪闻到酒香，也把头探到瓮中来喝。众人连忙张罗着把猪赶走，而阮咸却不介意，在猪中间挤过头去，和猪一起共饮起来。众人大笑，传为趣谈。

● 阮咸像
Portrait of Ruan Xian

Ruan Xian Drank with Hogs

Ruan Xian, courtesy name Zhongrong, a resident of Chenliu (near the present Kaifeng City of Henan Province), was praised together with Ji Kang, Ruan Ji, Shan Tao, Xiang Xiu, Liu Ling, and Wang Rong as "the Seven Sages of the Bamboo Grove". He was not only versed in music but also known for his carefree and unruly disposition, which had produced and left a number of interesting anecdotes to the world. There was a time when Ruan Xian was attending a clan gathering for the Ruan's, everyone present was so happy as to suggest replacing the small wine cups with bigger containers to satisfy their joyful feelings. Therefore, everyone sat around the wine jar and toasted to each others, when a pack of hogs in the nearby smelled the wine fragrance and came to stick their heads into the jar for wine. While everybody started up and managed to drive away the hogs, Ruan Xian didn't mind at all and kept making his way to the jar among the hogs in order to drink the wine. Everybody was in great laughter at the scene and spoke of it later as an interesting anecdote.

● 五彩竹林七贤图盘（清）
Five-colored Plate with the Picture of the Seven Sages of the Bamboo Grove (Qing Dynasty, 1644-1911)

三弦

三弦又称"弦子"，是中国传统的弹拨乐器。其柄很长，有方形音箱，两面蒙皮，张三根弦。音色豪迈粗犷，可以独奏、合奏或伴奏，普遍用于民族器乐、戏曲音乐和说唱音乐。

早在公元前214年，秦始皇灭六国完成统一后，就征发百姓去修筑万里长城。为了调剂繁重的劳役，北方各民族人民曾把一种有柄的小摇鼓加以改造，制成弹拨乐器，当时称为"弦鼗"。这就是三弦的前身，最早在北方边疆的军队中使用。宋元时期，三弦已广泛流传于全国各地。尤其是在元朝，三弦成为元曲的主要伴奏乐器，当时曾称"弦索"。

三弦又分为小三弦与大三弦两种。北方各种大鼓、单弦等曲艺，多用大三弦伴奏；南方的弹词类曲艺、昆曲等剧

Three-strings

Three-strings (*San Xian*), also known as *Xian Zi*, is a traditional Chinese plucked string instrument with a very long stem with three strings and a square sound box covered with skin on both sides. With unsophisticated and unrestrained sounds, three-strings can be played in solo, ensemble, or accompanying music, and is mostly performed in ethnic instrument music, opera music, and storytelling music.

In as early as 214 B.C. when the First Emperor of Qin conquered the six states and unified the whole China, people were recruited to build up the Great Wall. In order to alleviate the heavy burden from the hard labor, those people from the northern ethnic groups transformed a handled tambourine into a plucked string instrument called *Xian Tao*. *Xian Tao* was the predecessor of three-strings, and was used in the army in the northern frontier. In the Song Dynasty (960-1279) and Yuan Dynasty (1206-1368), three-strings

● 三弦
Three-strings

种，以及丝竹类器乐合奏，多用小三弦。

　　三弦因琴鼓两面都蒙以皮膜，声音极为独特动听。演奏三弦时采用坐姿，两腿自然分开，或将右腿搭在左腿上，琴鼓置于右腿上，琴头斜向左上方。左手轻扶琴杆，用食指、中指、无名指按弦，右手持拨片或戴甲套弹拨琴弦发音。由于三弦琴杆无品，弹奏时音域间高低变化自由，可奏出各种滑音，因此在所有的说唱、戏曲和歌唱伴奏

had prevailed all over the country. In the Yuan Dynasty in particular, it became the main accompanying instrument in Yuan songs and was once called *Xian Suo* at that time.

　　There are two kinds of three-strings: small three-strings and large three-strings. Most of the vocal arts of *Da Gu* (story-telling with drum accompaniment) and *Dan Xian* (story-telling with drum and three-strings accompaniment) in the north use the large three-strings for accompanying music, while those vocal arts in the south like *Tan Ci* (storytelling to the accompaniment of stringed instruments), the folk operas like *Kun Qu*, and the ensembles of silk and bamboo instruments mostly use small three-strings.

　　Since the both sides of three-strings' sound box are covered with a membrane of skin, it sounds more special and pleasant. The instrument is played in a sitting position with both legs setting naturally apart and then the right leg being placed over the left leg. The sound

● 弹三弦乐俑（元）
Figurine of Musician Playing Three-strings (Yuan Dynasty, 1206-1368)

box is put on the right lap with the head tilting toward the left. The left hand gently holds the pillar with the index finger, the middle finger, and the ring finger pressing the strings, while the right hand uses either a spectrum or stalled fingers to pluck the strings. Since the pillar of three-strings doesn't have frets, it allows more free play in the high or low sound between different diapasons, and is capable of producing glides, which makes it competent in serving as a foil in accompanying storytelling, operas and vocals. Especially in the transition of tunes, it is more agile and suitable for performing lyrical melodies or vehement tunes in full expressiveness.

中，都能很好地起到衬托作用，尤其在转调时更为灵活，最宜于演奏抒情的旋律和激昂的曲调，极具表现力。

苏州弹词与三弦

苏州弹词是流行于长江中下游地区的一种曲艺艺术，发源于明末清初的苏州，20世纪上半叶在上海达到鼎盛，受到江南百姓的普遍喜爱。在苏州弹词诞生之初，三弦和琵琶就是其伴奏乐器。苏州弹词以说为主，以唱为辅，演出形式以一人演出的"单档"和两人演出的"双档"为主。单档演员手持三弦，自弹自唱；双档演出时，坐在左边弹三弦的演员为"上手"，控制情节与节奏，右边持琵琶的为"下手"，配合上手演出。苏州弹词所用三弦比一般三弦小，亦称"书弦"，弹奏时不使用假指甲。弹词演员演出时，坐高椅，下有垫脚，双腿叠放，演唱时要收腹挺胸，以保持形体优美及演唱气息流畅。使用三弦伴唱时，三弦一般演奏骨干音，具有支撑作用，发挥其高音区灵活轻快、低音区浑厚稳重的特点，用细碎灵巧的旋律烘托唱腔。

Suzhou *Tan Ci* and Three-strings

Suzhou *Tan Ci* is a kind of vocal arts popular in the middle and lower reaches of Yangtze River, and originated in Suzhou at the end of the Ming Dynasty (1368-1644) and beginning of the Qing Dynasty (1644-1911). In the first half of the 20th century, it reached its summit in Shanghai and was widely favored by people in Jiangnan, that is, the regions south of Yangtze River. When Suzhou *Tan Ci* first rose, three-strings and pear-shaped lute were the main accompanying instruments. Suzhou *Tan Ci* is based primarily on speaking and supplemented by singing. The performance takes forms of either a one-man show called *Dan Dang* or a two-man show, *Shuang Dang*. The *Dan Dang* performer holds the instrument while playing and singing simultaneously; in the *Shuang Dang* performance, the person sitting on the left, called "upper hand" (*Shang Shou*), plays three-strings and controls the story and the beats, while the one on the right playing pear-shaped lute, called "lower hand" (*Xia Shou*), plays in keeping with the upper hand. The instrument used in Suzhou *Tan Ci* is a little smaller than the ordinary three-strings, called *Shu Xian*. No fingerstalls are needed for it. When the *Tan Ci* players perform, they sit on high chairs with their foot landing on the foot-rest of the chair, leg crossed, and have to keep their torso straight and belly sucked in to maintain the physical poise as well as unblocked breathing channel. In performances, three-strings is usually used to play the backbone sounds for supporting functions so that it can fully play out its special features of fast and lively treble as well as thick and steady bass, with subtle and dextrous rhythms to set off the singing tune.

● 苏州弹词的演出
Performance of Suzhou *Tan Ci*

扬琴

扬琴是一种发源于中东地区的击弦乐器，公元12、13世纪在东欧各国十分流行。明朝万历年间，随着中国和西方日趋密切的友好往来，扬琴由波斯经海路传入中国，最初只流行在广东一带，后来逐渐扩散到中国各地。当时被称为"洋琴"，又因为它的琴箱形状像蝴蝶，被称为"蝴蝶琴"。扬琴传入中国后，在许多地方戏曲和曲艺中得到采用，如粤剧、闽剧、沪剧、

Dulcimer

Dulcimer (*Yang Qin*) is a hammered string instrument which originated in the Middle East and became popular in east European countries in the 12th and 13th centuries. During the Wanli Period (1573-1620) of Ming Dynasty (1368-1644) as the friendly communication between China and the western countries grew frequent, dulcimer was introduced into China through waterways from Persia. It was initially popular only in Guandong and later scattered through all over China. It was at first called *Yang Qin*, *Yao Qin*, or butterfly *Qin* because of the resemblance of its sound box to the shape of a butterfly. After dulcimer was introduced into China, it was applied in many folk operas and vocal arts, such as Yue opera, Min opera, Lu opera, Yang opera, Han opera, and so on. Many local vocal arts are also named after dulcimer (*Yang Qin*), such as Shandong *Qin Shu*, Sichuan *Yang Qin*, Beijing *Qin Shu*, and so forth. After being carried on and developed

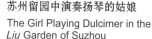

苏州留园中演奏扬琴的姑娘
The Girl Playing Dulcimer in the *Liu* Garden of Suzhou

马子，呈条形峰谷状，用竹、红木或牛骨制作，有两至五个，置于面板上，左侧的为高音马，右侧为低音马，其凸出的峰部用以架弦，凹下的谷部为其他琴弦通过。

The bridges are made with strips of bamboo, redwood or cow bone which curves up and down (in the shape of a wave). There are 2 to 5 bridges on the front panel. Those on the left are high-pitch bridges and those on the left are low-pitch bridges. The parts that curve up are used to prop up the strings while the recessed parts allow other strings to go through.

琴弦，最早用铜丝弦，现采用钢丝弦。高音部分为裸弦，低音部分用缠弦，在裸弦上缠绕细钢丝而成。

The strings were originally made of copper, but are now made of steel. The strings for playing the treble are bare strings and those for the bass, twined strings, are bare strings intertwined with slimmer, fine steel wires.

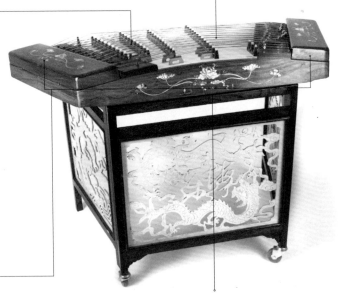

山口，面板两侧的长形木条，用红木制成，起架弦作用，山口至马子的一段弦，才是琴弦的振动发音部分。

The saddles are the wood strips located on both sides of the front panel. Made of redwood, they function as the supports for the strings, propping them up. The section on the strings located between the saddle and bridge, is the area which produces vibrations and sounds.

共鸣箱，由前后两块侧板和左右两端琴头连接成琴架，上下蒙以薄板而成。

The resonator box is composed of two side-boards on the front and back sides, and is connected with the dulcimer heads located on both the right and left ends, forming the dulcimer stand, while the top and the bottom are covered with thin boards.

● **扬琴**（图片提供：全景正片）

Dulcimer

扬剧、汉剧等都是用扬琴伴奏，而且不少民间曲艺还以"扬琴"命名，如山东琴书、四川扬琴、北京琴书等。在中国经过400年的流传和民间艺人的不断改造，扬琴不论在乐器制作、演奏艺术还是乐曲创作上，都已具有中国传统特色和民族风格。

扬琴在演奏时，琴置于架上，演奏者左右手各执一琴竹分别敲击条码两侧的琴弦，竹法（即演奏技巧）非常灵活多样，便于表现轻快、活泼的曲调。

in China for 400 years, Dulcimer has been so much transformed by folk artists that either in the manufacture of the instrument or in its performance and musical creation, it has taken on Chinese traditional features as well as ethnic styles.

In performances, dulcimer is placed on a stand with the performer holding a bamboo hammers in each hand hammering on the strings on both sides of the bridge. Its playing skills are flexible and diversified and serve well those fast and lively tunes.

中国乐器大家族 The Extended Family of Chinese Musical Instruments

北京琴书

琴书是一种民间传统说唱艺术形式，因演唱时以扬琴为主要伴奏乐器而得名。琴书种类很多，起源不一，大多是由当地民歌、小调发展而成。北京琴书形成于20世纪40年代，源于河北廊坊及北京郊区，流行于北京、天津、河北等地。琴书的表演形式是一人站唱，以左手敲击铁片，右手执鼓楗击扁鼓，以三弦、四胡、扬琴等乐器伴奏。唱腔借鉴了另一种说唱曲种——京韵大鼓转圜自然的风格技巧，"说似唱、唱似说"，唱腔中夹用说白，突出表现北京土言土语，板式丰富、旋律简洁，表演和演唱风格生动活泼，深受百姓喜爱。

Beijing *Qin Shu*

The *Qin Shu* is a traditional folk art-form of storytelling. It is mainly accompanied by dulcimer music in its performance, which is where gains its name. There is a multitude of different *Qin Shu*, each of which has a different origin. Most of them were developments from local folk songs, small tunes or ditties. Beijing *Qin Shu* originated in Langfang in the Hebei Province and the suburbs of Beijing during the 40s of the 20th century, and popularized in Beijing, Tianjin, Hebei and other places. The performance of *Qin Shu* involves a person singing in the standing position, with their left hand clapping iron plates and the right hand holding a drumstick to beat a flat drum to the accompaniment of the music made by the three-strings, the *Si Hu* (four-stringed zither with strings tuned in pairs), the dulcimer, and the like. The "singing" tune is borrowed from another kind of storytelling, *Jing Yun Da Gu*, which has a more "natural" style as well as more "natural" techniques; This style features a "telling like singing and singing like telling" as well as "plain talks" inserted in the singing, highlighting the local Beijing dialects. It has rich meter forms, concise rhythms and lively singing styles, thus it is deeply favored by common people.

冬不拉

冬不拉，是起源于中亚地区的传统弹拨乐器，在新疆的哈萨克族中尤其流行。冬不拉的琴杆细长，音箱有瓢形和扁平两种，一般用松木、桦木或桑木制作，雕刻精细，镶嵌美观琴颈多用整木斫成。琴弦过去用羊肠制成，多为两根，也有三根的，现已改用尼龙缠钢丝弦代替，并在琴颈上增加了铜质的品位。

演奏冬不拉时，需将琴斜置于怀中，左手持琴按弦，右手弹拨，主要用中指和拇指拨弦，有时也使用拨片弹奏。冬不拉音量不大，但音色优雅。演奏者运用不同的演奏方法，可生动地再现草原上众多声音，如淙淙的流水声、婉转的鸟鸣声、羊群的欢腾声以及骏马疾行的

Dombura

The dombura (*Dong Bu La*) is a plucked string instrument which originated in Central Asia and popularized mainly among the Kazakh ethnic group of Xinjiang. The dombura has a slender and long body, and has either a gourd-ladle-shaped or oblate-shaped sound box. It is usually made of pine wood, birch wood, or mulberry wood with delicate sculptures and magnificent inlays. Its neck is carved out of a whole woodblock. There are two or three strings, which used to be made of goat intestines in the past, but are now steel wires intertwined with nylon threads. On the neck there are added frets made of copper.

When the dombura is played, it is held diagonally to the chest with the fingers of the left hand pressing the

冬不拉的传说

  传说在很早以前，草原上有一个残暴的可汗。他的儿子在一次狩猎中失踪，可汗下令必须在三天内找到他，不过谁带来不好的消息，将会受到残酷的惩罚。一个年轻的骑手在一棵树旁发现了可汗儿子的尸体。可是，怎么向可汗报告这件事呢？他找到了草原上最聪明的老牧人，请他帮忙出主意。老人苦思了好久，终于想出了办法。他从树上锯下两块最好的薄木板，又宰杀了自己的马，抽出马腿上的两条长筋，做成了一把神奇的乐器。老人来到王宫，拿出赶制的乐器对着可汗弹起来，凄美的乐声如实地讲述了事情的经过。可汗听完暴跳如雷，要将老人投入铝水沸腾的锅中。老人镇定地告诉可汗，发出声音的是手中的乐器"冬不拉"。可汗失去理智，命令武士抓捕老人，老人又拿起冬不拉，唱起了心底深藏已久的积愤。老人的歌使武士们个个义愤填膺，不由得跟着老人一起高唱。愤怒的歌声把可汗吓瘫了，他从高高的王位上摔下来，掉进了沸腾的铝水里。从此以后，哈萨克人民心灵的伙伴——冬不拉便在草原上流行开了。

The Legend of Dombura

Legend has it that long time ago, there was a cruel Khan ruling the grassland. One day, his son went missing during a hunt. The Khan ordered the people to find him in three days. Anyone who brought unpleasant news would receive brutal punishment. A young rider found the body of the Khan's son, but didn't know how he should report this to the Khan. He sought advice from the wisest old shepherd in the grassland and consulted with him. After musing for a while, the old man finally came up with an idea. He cut out two fine boards from the tree, killed his horse, drew out two long sinews from the horse legs, and made a wonder musical instrument. The old man went to the palace and started to play music with the roughly made instrument. The beautiful yet sad melody expressed what had happened. After hearing it, the Khan threw a tantrum and wanted to throw the old man into a cauldron of boiling water. The old man calmly told the Khan that it was the dombura, the instrument in his hand, which told the bad news. However, the Khan, out of his mind, ordered his soldiers to seize the old man when the old man picked up his dombura and began to let out all the buried indignation within the depths of his heart. His song moved the soldiers, feeling his indignation, and sang along with the old man. The angry song frightened the Khan so much that he fell from his throne and plunged into the boiling cauldron. Ever since then, the dombura has become the "bosom partner" of the Kazakh people and grew as a popular instrument amongst the people living in the grassland.

● 冬不拉
Dombura

● 弹冬不拉的老人（图片提供：FOTOE）
The Old Man Playing Dombura

蹄声等。

　　冬不拉弹唱是哈萨克族人最喜爱的表演形式，演唱者既可自弹自唱，也可用于独奏或乐器合奏，表现力十分丰富。而且它轻巧便，便于携带，适合草原人民多迁徙的生活，故深受人们的喜爱。

热瓦普

　　热瓦普，又称"拉瓦波"、"喇巴卜"等，是新疆维吾尔族、乌孜别克族的一种弹拨乐器。琴身为木制，音箱为半球形，以羊皮、驴皮、马皮

strings while the thumb and middle finger of the right hand, or a plectrum in some cases, to pluck the strings. The dombura doesn't produce loud sounds but it still sounds beautiful. With different playing skills, it can picturesquely play out the sounds of a running fountain in the grassland, crisp bird chirping, jubilant hoof sounds of sheep groups or speedy steeds.

Playing and singing with the dombura is a favorite way of performing by the Kazakh people. The performer can play and sing at the same time, or use the dombura in solo performances or in instrument ensembles having rich expressions. It is lightweight, convenient to carry along, which is suitable for the migrating lifestyle for those living on the grassland, and therefore deeply loved by people.

Rubab

The rubab, also known as the "robab", among other names, is a plucked string instrument popular amongst the Uygur and Ozbek ethnic groups in Xinjiang. Its body is made of wood; the sound box is made in the shape of a hemisphere and is covered with the skin of a goat, a mule,

或蟒皮蒙面；琴颈细长，顶部弯曲，张五根金属弦，多个音品。热瓦普的音色响亮，多用于合奏与伴奏，亦可作为独奏乐器使用。独奏乐曲多为木卡姆或民歌的曲调。

热瓦普按形制、流行地区、定弦方式及演奏方式，可分为喀什热瓦普、乌孜别克热瓦普、多兰热瓦普等几种。

喀什热瓦普因流行于新疆喀什地区而得名，曾为清代宫廷"回部乐"的乐器之一。琴长一百三十厘米，指板上缠有二十八个丝弦品。音箱半球形，蒙羊皮、驴皮或蟒皮。张一根金属主奏弦，四至七根共鸣弦。演奏时乐器横置胸前，以右手腕夹持音箱，拇指、食指执牛角片或塑料拨子弹奏，左手扶琴颈并按弦。外弦奏旋律，共鸣弦奏低音或和音。

乌孜别克热瓦普是据喀什热瓦普改造而成，又称"改良热瓦普"，是在喀什热瓦普的基础上缩短琴杆，加大共鸣箱，取消共鸣弦。指板上按十二平均律设置铜品。张四至五根金属弦。音色比喀什热瓦普明亮，音域更宽。演奏方

a horse, or a python; the neck is long and slender with its top curved. It has 5 metal strings and multiple frets. The sounds the rubab makes is loud and vibrant and is used mostly in chord or accompaniment. It can be used as a solo instrument or for the tunes of the Maqams or folk songs.

In accordance with its shape, the origin of its popularity, the style of string tuning and the playing method, the rubab can be divided into several types such as the Kashgar rubab, Ozbek rubab, Dolan rubab, and so forth.

The Kashgar rubab is named in accordance to its popularity in the Kashgar areas of Xinjiang. It was listed as an instrument used for "Hui People's Music" in the court of the Qing Dynasty (1644-1911). It's 130 cm long, with 28 silk frets twined on the finger board. The sound box is made in the shape of a hemisphere, covered with the skin of a goat, a mule or a python. There is one presiding string made of metal, among 4 to 7 resonance strings. When it is played, the instrument is laid transversely in front of the chest, with the right wrist clamping the sound box and the thumb and index finger holding a plectrum, made from a bulls' horn or plastic, to pluck the strings, while the left hand holding its

中国乐器大家族

The Extended Family of Chinese Musical Instruments

法与喀什热瓦普基本相同，更便于奏和音、和弦。

多兰热瓦普又译为"刀朗热瓦普"，流行于新疆巴楚、阿瓦提、麦盖提、莎车等地。其体积较大，音箱有葫芦形、圆形等多种。琴杆短而粗，张三根金属主奏弦、七至十根金属共鸣弦。演奏时琴置于右腿，左手持琴按弦，右手持拨子弹奏。

• 弹奏热瓦普的维吾尔族老人（图片提供：FOTOE）
A Uygur Old Man Playing a Rubab

neck and pressing on the strings. The outer strings are for rhythms and the resonance strings are for bass and chords.

The Ozbek rubab, also called "innovated rubab", is an innovated version of Kashgar rubab, with pillar shortened, resonator box enlarged, and resonance strings cancelled. Copper frets are installed on the finger board in accordance with the 12 equal temperament. It has 4 to 5 metal strings, producing brighter timbre and broader range than Kashgar rubab. Its playing method is basically the same with the Kashgar rubab, but is easier for accord and chords.

The Dolan rubab, or "Doran rubab" in different translations, is popular in places such as Patrul, Awati, Makit, Shache and other places in Xinjiang. It is big in size and the sound box is made in the shape of a gourd, a ball or other similar shapes. The body is short and thick, with 3 metal presiding strings and 7 to 10 metal resonance strings. When it is played, the instrument is placed on the right lap, with the left hand holding it and pressing on the strings, while the right hand using a plectrum to pluck the strings.

> 打击乐器

打击乐器是一种以打、摇动、摩擦、刮等方式产生音响的乐器类别。在中国传统乐器中，打击乐器具有非常悠久的历史。其中有些是有固定音高的打击乐器，如云锣、编钟等。此外还有一些是无固定音高的，如拍板、梆子、鼓等。

钟

钟最早是古人祭祀或宴飨时用的打击乐器，由商代的铙演变而来，始于西周中期，沿用至今。秦汉以后，钟成为打点定时和警示用的响器。钟可分为甬钟、纽钟、镈钟三类。无论哪类钟，其基本形制皆为扁圆体，平顶，顶上有可悬挂的纽。

商代以后，器乐演奏用的钟往往成组出现，每组内三枚至数十枚不

> Percussion Instrument

The percussion instrument is in a category of instruments which use the methods of hitting, shaking, rubbing, scraping and so on to generate musical effects. Among the traditional Chinese musical instruments, the percussion instrument has witnessed a very long history. Some of them have a fixed high-pitched sound, such as cloud gongs (*Yun Luo*), serials bells (*Bian Zhong*) and the like; others have no fixed high pitch, like clappers (*Pai Ban*), wooden stick (*Bang Zi*), drums, and so on.

Bell

The bell (Zhong) was a percussion instrument used by ancient people for worship or banquets. It was derived from the cymbals (*Nao*) from the Shang Dynasty (1600 B.C.-1046 B.C.), and has been used since the beginning of the Mid-

传统乐器
Traditional Chinese Musical Instruments

• 虢季甬钟（西周）
Column Bell of Guoji (Western Zhou Dynasty, 1046 B.C.-771 B.C.)

• 秦公钟（春秋）
Qingong Bell (Spring and Autumn Period, 770 B.C.-476 B.C.)

等，称为"编钟"。早在3500年前，中国就有了编钟，不过最早的编钟多为三枚一套。后来随着时代的发展，每套编钟的个数也不断增加。1978年

Western Zhou Dynasty (1046 B.C.-771 B.C.) up to now. After the Qin Dynasty (221 B.C.-206 B.C.) and the Han Dynasty (206 B.C.- 220 A.D.), the bell became an instrument for time-telling or alerting people. The bell can be divided into three kinds: the column bell, the knot bell, and the *Bo* bell. Whichever kind it is, the basic form of bell is an oblate body with a flat top, where a knob is cast onto it for hanging.

After the Shang Dynasty, performance bell appeared in rows, with 3 to 10 pieces of bell arranged in a row, called the serials bells (*Bian Zhong*). As early as 3,500 years ago, the serials bells appeared, mostly with 3 bells in a row. As it developed over time, the number of bells in each set in the serials bells increased. The Marquis Yi of Zeng's serials bells, unearthed from his tomb in *Leigudun*, in the southern suburbs of Suizhou, Hubei Province, is so far the largest set of serials bells, composing of 65 pieces, which may cover up a whole stage in a modern music hall. The sounds produced by the serials bells are based on the size of the body. The smaller the body the higher the pitch, but with a softer volume; the bigger the body the lower the pitch while having a louder

● **曾侯乙编钟（战国）** （图片提供：全景正片）

这套编钟出土于湖北省随州市南郊擂鼓墩的曾侯乙墓，由六十五件青铜编钟组成，其音域跨五个半八度，十二个半音齐备。这套完整的编钟以大小和音高为序编成八组悬挂在三层钟架上。最上层三组十九件为钮钟，中下两层五组共四十五件为甬钟，有长柄，钟体遍饰浮雕式蟠虺纹，细密精致，钟上有错金铭文。这是我国迄今发现数量最多、保存最好、音律最全、气势最宏伟的一套编钟，它深埋地下2400余年，至今仍能演奏乐曲，音律准确，音色优美，堪称稀世珍宝。

The Marquis Yi of Zeng's Serials Bells (Warring States Period, 476 B.C.-221 B.C.)

This large set of serials bells, unearthed from the Tomb of the Marquis Yi of Zeng at *Leigudun* in the southern suburbs of Suizhou, Hubei Province, is composed of 65 pieces of bronze bells, the diapason of which covers a range of five half-octaves and a full dozen semitones. This entire set of serials bells is arranged in 8 groups in accordance to sizes and the pitch sounds they produce, and is hung on a rack having three levels. On the top level are the 18 pieces of knot bells arranged into three groups; on the middle and lower levels are 45 pieces of column bells arranged into 5 groups. The long-handled body of the bell is decorated with an exquisite and detailed Pan Hui (coiled dragons or snakes) pattern in relief with gold-inlaid inscriptions. Currently, it is the most magnificent set of serials bells that has ever been discovered, having the most pieces, kept in the best condition, and having the most complete sound scales. Although it was buried underground for over 2,400 years, it can still be played with in-tune and beautiful tones. It deserves its title of being a rare treasure of the world.

• 大晟铜钟（北宋）
Dacheng Bronze Bell
(Northern Song Dynasty,
960-1127)

出土于湖北随州南郊擂鼓墩曾侯乙墓的曾侯乙编钟，是至今为止所发现的最大一套编钟，共六十五件，足以占满一个现代音乐厅的整个舞台。编钟的发声原理大体是，钟体小，音调就高，音量也小；钟体大，音调就低，音量也大，所以铸造时的尺寸和形状对编钟有重要的影响。古代的编钟多用于宫廷的演奏，在民间很少流传，每逢征战、朝见或祭祀等活动时，都要演奏编钟。

磬

磬是古代石制的一种打击乐器。一般认为，磬是由石锄、石犁一类的农具演化而来。原始社会的人们在劳作之余偶然敲响石犁，发现音色悦耳，于是劳动工具就逐渐演变成了乐器。20世纪70年代在山西夏县东下冯遗址出土了一件大石

volume. Therefore, the size and the shape that the bell is the key factor in the sounds it produces. In the ancient times, the serials bells were played in the court, and were seldom seen in local society. They are played on occasions of warfare, in court meetings, in rituals and so on.

Musical Stone

Musical stone (Qing) is an ancient percussion instrument made of stone. It is believed to have evolved from farmer's tools such as a stone hoe or stone plough. In the primitive society, people accidentally found the beautiful sounds produced by knocking on the stone plough during their break between working on the farm. The farming tool eventually evolved into a musical instrument. In 1970s, a big musical stone was discovered at the archeological site of the *Dongxiafeng* Ruins in Xia County, Shanxi Province. The musical stone is

磬，长60厘米，上部有一穿孔，击之声音悦耳。经测定，此磬距今约4000年，属于夏代的遗存，这是迄今发现最早的磬的实物。

在商代，磬的制作已十分精美，并为宫廷乐队所专用。为王室宫廷乐队所用。按照使用场所和演奏方式，磬可以分为特磬和编磬两种：特磬是皇帝祭祀天地和祖先

60cm long with a hole in the upper part and produces pleasant sounds. According to the measurement, it was made approximately 4,000 years ago during the Xia Dynasty (2070 B.C.-1600 B.C.). It's the oldest artifact of musical stone that has ever been uncovered.

In the Shang Dynasty (1600 B.C.-1046 B.C.), musical stone had been widely used. Delicately crafted, musical stone was used in the imperial families by court musical bands. Based on its performance sites and playing methods, musical stone can be classified into special musical stone and musical stone formation. Special musical stone is an instrument used by emperors in rituals in the worship of heaven, earth or ancestors; Musical stone formation is a group of a certain number of musical stones hung on a wooden rack for playing, and is used mainly in court music. In 1978, a set of musical stone formation was unearthed from the Tomb of the Marquis Yi of Zeng in Suizhou, Hubei Province. There are 32 musical stones in total hung orderly in two levels on a bronze rack with exquisite animal patterns on the bottom and dragon heads on the top. In the Qing Dynasty (1644-1911), the musical stone formation was mainly used in celebrations and ceremonies held by

时演奏的乐器；编磬是若干个磬编成一组，挂在木架上演奏，主要用于宫廷音乐。1978年，湖北随州曾侯乙墓出土了战国初年的一套石编磬，共三十二枚，原分上下两层，依次悬挂于精美的兽座龙首铜架上。清代的编磬，主要用于皇帝与王公大臣的庆典、宫中大型宴会。清乾隆年间制作的编磬，十六枚为一套，大小相同，厚度有异，采用新疆和田碧玉，其形与特磬一致，只是体积较小，每次演奏时全套都要使用，随乐曲旋律击奏。乾隆五十五年（1790年），乾隆皇帝还用黄金制作了一套金编磬，和一套金编钟一起使用。

the emperor, the imperial princes and court ministers, or in the grand banquets hosted in the imperial court. The musical stone formation crafted during the reign of Emperor Qianlong (1736-1795) in the Qing Dynasty has 16 same-sized musical stones in a set but different thickness, made of the jade produced in Hetian, Xinjiang. Their shapes are consistent with those of special musical stone but with a smaller size. For performance, all the musical stones in the set is to be used for hitting in accordance with the melody. In the 55th year of Qianlong's reign (1790), Emperor Qianlong used gold to craft a set of gold musical stones and a set of gold serials bells for ensembles.

• 湖南长沙马王堆汉墓出土的木编磬（西汉）
Wood Musical Stone Formation Unearthed in the *Mawangdui* Tomb of the Han Dynasty, in Changsha, Hunan Province (Western Han Dynasty, 206 B.C.- 25 A.D.)

鼓

　　鼓是中国传统的打击乐器，一般是在坚固的圆桶形鼓身的一面或双面蒙上一块拉紧的皮膜，用手或鼓槌敲击出声。据记载，在远古时期的传说中就出现了陶土做的鼓。由于鼓有良好的共鸣作用，声音高亢雄浑、传声很远，所以很早就用来为军队战阵助威。相传黄帝征服蚩尤的涿鹿之战中，"黄帝杀蚩尤，以其皮为鼓，声闻五百"。到了周代，朝廷专门建立了管理鼓乐

Drum

Drum (*Gu*) is a traditional Chinese percussion instrument. It usually has a solid barrel-like body with one side or both sides covered with a tensioned skin membrane, hammered by hands or drumsticks. According to the recorded legend, ceramic drums already appeared in the remotest antiquity. Since drums have a very good resonance effect, and produce inspiring, sturdy, powerful, and far-reaching sounds, they have long been used in military battlefields for cheering for the soldiers. It was said in the Battle

• 新石器时代红陶鼓（仰韶文化）
Red Ceramic Drum of the Neolithic Era (*Yangshao* Culture, around 5000 B.C-3000 B.C.)

• 击鼓乐伎纹玉带板（唐）
Jade Belt Linked to Board with a Drumming Musician (Tang Dynasty, 618-907)

三彩骑马击鼓俑（唐）
Tricolored Figurine of the Drumming
Horse Rider (Tang Dynasty, 618-907)

的机构，设置了专管鼓事的官职
"鼓人"，并制定了一套鼓乐的制
度。当时的鼓主要用于祭祀，如用
于祭天的鼓称为"雷鼓"，祭地的
鼓称为"灵鼓"，祭祖的鼓称为
"路鼓"。隋唐时期，随着民族的
大融合，许多少数民族的鼓传入中
原，汇集到宫廷之中，如羯鼓、齐
鼓、答腊鼓等，大多为细腰形的
鼓，用鼓腔周边的绳索调节鼓皮的
张力。

of Zhuolu where the Yellow Emperor
defeated Chiyou, the "Yellow Emperor
killed Chiyou and used his skin for
the drum, the sound of which could be
transmitted five hundred miles away." In
the Zhou Dynasty (1046 B.C.-256 B.C.),
the imperial court established a specific
organization in charge of the management
of drums, appointed a man as the official
to administer the affairs of drums, called
"drum person" and set up a system of
drum music. At that time, the drum was
mainly used in rituals. For example, the
drum used in the ritual in the worship of
heaven was called "thunder drum"; those
worshiping the earth called "spiritual
drum"; and those worshiping their
ancestors called "road drum". In the Sui
Dynasty (581-618) and Tang Dynasty
(618-907), as various ethnic groups fused
together in development, many of the
drums from different ethnic minorities
were introduced to the Central Plains
and eventually gathered in the imperial
court, such as *Jie* drum, *Qi* drum and *Da
La* drum. Most of them were shaped with
a narrow waist and used the cord around
the drum chamber to adjust the tension of
the drum skin.

腰鼓

　　腰鼓在公元4世纪时开始流行，其形似圆筒，两端略细，中间稍粗，两端蒙皮，鼓身有两只铁环，用带子悬挂在腰间，两手各执一木槌敲打，无固定音高，音响清亮，既可用作伴舞乐器，也可作为舞蹈道具，表现欢快热闹的情景。

Waist Drum

Waist drum began to prevail in the 4th century. It looks like a tube with both ends a little narrower than the middle part. Skin covers both ends and the drum body has two iron rings attached so they can be tied to the waist through a robe. Both skin-covered surfaces are to be hammered by wood mallets. It doesn't

• 击腰鼓者砖雕（五代）
Brick Sculpture of Waist Drum Player (Five Dynasties, 907-960)

渔鼓

渔鼓又称"竹琴"或"道筒"，南宋时已经出现。现代使用的渔鼓，是在长65～100厘米、直径13厘米左右的竹筒上，一端蒙以猪皮或羊皮而成。演奏时，左手竖抱渔鼓，右手拍击。和渔鼓一起使用的还有简板，用

● **黄慎《八仙图》（清）**

八仙是中国道教传说中的八位神仙，其中有一位张果老，常见的形象就是抱着渔鼓、倒骑着毛驴。传说他常常云游四方，敲打着渔鼓、简板，演唱道情，劝化世人。

Picture of the Eight Immortals by Huang Shen (Qing Dynasty, 1644-1911) (with Zhang Guolao being partially enlarged)

The Eight Immortals are the legendary figures of Chinese Taoism. One of them is Zhang Guolao, usually seen holding a fisher drum and riding a mule in reverse. Legend has it that he was always traveling around, hammering a fisher drum, clapping a *Jian Ban* and singing *Dao Qing* to preach to the people.

have fixed treble but has clear and bright sounds. It can be used to accompany dance or be used as a dancing tool to express joy for an occasion.

Fisher Drum

Fisher drum, also called *Zhu Qin* or *Dao Tong*, appeared in the Southern Song Dynasty (1127-1279). Modern fisher drum is a bamboo tube of 65 to 100 cm in length and about 13 cm in diameter, with one end covered with the skin of a pig or sheep. When it is played, the left hand holds the fisher drum vertically while the

竹片制作，长45~65厘米，一端向外弯曲，两根为一副。演奏时用左手夹击发音，与渔鼓一起为"渔鼓"、"道情"伴奏。渔鼓是民间曲艺"道情"、"渔鼓"和"竹琴"的主要伴奏乐器。

堂鼓

又称"同鼓"，以木为框，两面蒙牛皮。演奏时，将鼓放在木架上，用双木槌敲击。堂鼓鼓面较大，从鼓心到鼓边可以发出音高、音色不同的声音，一般是鼓心的音

• 击鼓散乐砖雕（宋）
Brick Sculpture of Drummer's Musical Performance (Song Dynasty, 960-1279)

right hand hits it. Fisher drum is usually accompanied by *Jian Ban*, a pair of bamboo plates 45 to 65 cm long with one end curved outward. In a performance, the player uses the left hand to hit *Jian Ban* in combination with fisher drum to serve as accompanying music for *Yu Gu* and *Dao Qing* (forms of folk art). Fisher drum is the key accompanying instrument in the performance of the folk vocal arts of *Dao Qing*, *Yu Gu* and *Zhu Qin*.

Tang Drum

Also known as *Tong* drum, *Tang* drum has a wooden frame covered with cow skin on both sides. When it is played, the instrument is placed on a wood stand to be hammered by a pair of wood mallets. *Tang* drum has a vast skin surface, every part of which from the center to the rim can deliver different pitches timbres. Generally speaking, the center part produces lower sounds and the rim gives higher sounds. A great contrast in the volume and timbre can be produced by hitting the center or the rim as well as by the controlled force of hammering. It can also perform complicated styles to play up the atmosphere and emotions. *Tang* drum is a very common percussion instrument in folk music ensembles and opera music.

● 击鼓者砖雕（五代）
Brick Sculpture of Drummers (Five Dynasties, 907-960)

比较低，鼓边的音比较高。通过敲击鼓边、鼓心和控制敲击力度，可以获得大幅度的音量和音色对比，也能演奏出复杂的花点，对情绪及气氛的渲染有较大的作用，是民间器乐合奏及戏曲音乐中常用的一种打击乐器。

Shu Drum

The body of *Shu* drum is in oblate shape with both sides covered with skin. The skin face is 22 cm in diameter and the drum is 8.5 cm tall. It has lower sounds than *Tang* drum but a louder volume. Specifically used for accompanying music in the storytelling music of various *Gu Shu* (another name of *Da Gu*), such

书鼓

书鼓的鼓身呈扁圆形，两面蒙皮，鼓面直径22厘米，鼓身高8.5厘米，发音较堂鼓低，但很响亮，专用于北方说唱音乐"大鼓书"等各种鼓书伴奏，也适用于各地的曲艺演唱和鼓书伴奏。演奏时，书鼓置于竹制鼓架的编绳上，说唱演员左手执书板或梨花片，右手执鼓箭击鼓表演。

as *Da Gu Shu* in north China. *Shu* drum is also suitable as accompanying music for various vocal arts. When it is played, the instrument is placed on the robes on a stand made of bamboo, with the storytelling performer's left hand holding the clappers or pear-flower clappers, while the right hand uses the *Gu Jian* (a kind of drum stick used for one-sided drums) to hammer the drum.

中国乐器大家族 The Extended Family of Chinese Musical Instruments

● 京韵大鼓表演（图片提供：FOTOE）
Performance of *Jing Yun Da Gu*

板鼓

　　板鼓是形体矮小的单面鼓，鼓身由5块较厚的木板拼合而成，表面绝大部分是木制板面，中间振动发音的鼓面较小。其发音的部位是蒙皮的鼓腔部分，即所谓的"鼓光"。鼓腔的大小和蒙皮的松紧决定了板鼓发音的高低。为了保持鼓皮的张力，一般钉较多鼓钉，并在底部箍以铁圈。演奏时，将板鼓吊于木架上，用两根藤或竹制鼓箭敲击，鼓心、鼓边发音高低有别，使用不同敲击技巧，发音也不同。在戏曲乐队中，板鼓和拍板并用，由一人兼奏，居于领奏地位。

• 板鼓
Ban Drum

Ban Drum

Ban drum is a short and one-sided drum, whose body is pieced together by five thick wood plates. Most of the drum surface is made of wood panels. The resonating center on the drum surface is small, while the drum chamber is covered with skin, called *Gu Guang*, and is the major hammering spot for making sounds. The high and low pitch of *Ban* drum is decided by the size of the drum chamber and the tension of the drum skin. In order to maintain the tension of the drum skin, more drum nails are pounded into the body to hold the skin tight and the tension is enforced again by installing an iron plate around the drum at the bottom. When the drum is played, the instrument is hung on a wooden rack and hammered by a pair of *Gu Jian*, which are made of either cane or bamboo. In addition to the sound variety between the center part and the rim, the drum can also give different sounds with different hammering skills applied. In an opera band, *Ban* drum and clapper are usually used together and played by a single person in the position of leader.

铜鼓

铜鼓是流行于中国广西、广东、云南、贵州、四川、湖南等少数民族地区的一种打击乐器，最早出现于春秋晚期，自汉代以来十分常见。铜鼓全用铜铸，一般鼓面直径50厘米左右，高约30厘米，鼓腔中空，两侧有环状铜耳，全身都有精致的花纹。在历史上，铜鼓曾作为军鼓，少数民族的贵族也曾以占有铜鼓的多少作为权力的象征。不

Copper Drum

Copper drum is a percussion instrument popular among the ethnic groups in Guangxi, Guangdong, Yunnan, Guizhou, Sichuan, Hunan and other places. It first appeared in late Spring and Autumn Period (770 B.C.-476 B.C.), and became popular after the Han Dynasty (206 B.C.-220 A.D.). Copper drum is cast in copper and is about 30 cm in height with a drumming surface of 50 cm in diameter. The drum body is hollow with a pair of

- **五铢钱纹鼓（东汉）**
  鼓身上用汉代流通货币"五铢钱"捺印的纹样做装饰，说明两汉时西南各族和汉族在经济交往、文化融合上有密切关系。
  Wu Zhu-coin Drum (Eastern Han Dynasty, 25-220)

  The body of the instrument is decorated with the pattern of the "*Wu Zhu*" coin prints. It shows evidence that the ethnic groups in southwestern China had close ties with Han people in economic exchange and cultural fusion during the Han Dynasty (206 B.C.- 220 A.D.).

- **铜鼓（宋）**
  Copper Drum (Song Dynasty, 960-1279)

过铜鼓更多还是作为乐器，壮族、苗族至今还流传着铜鼓舞。

朝鲜族长鼓

朝鲜族长鼓又称"杖鼓"，是朝鲜族传统的打击乐器。鼓身为圆形、木制，两端鼓腔粗而中空，中间鼓腰细而实心，形似两个倒接的脚杯。左端与右端鼓腔大小不同，蒙皮也有分别，因而可以发出两种不同的音色，还能根据演奏的需要

rings on both sides. The body is decorated with delicate patterns. Copper drum was once used in military backgrounds. The aristocrats of some ethnic groups also used the number of the copper drum they owned to symbolize the power they had. However, copper drum is basically used as a musical instrument. The ethnic group of Zhuang and Miao still retain their traditional copper drum dance.

Korean Tambourin

The Korean tambourin, also known as *Zhang Gu*, is a traditional percussion instrument of the Korean ethnic people. The round body of the tambourin is made of wood with both ends of the body being thick and hollow while the waist of it is slim and solid, looking like an hourglass. The tambourin body on the left differs from that on the right, not only in size but also in the skin it is covered with. Therefore, the sounds made are different. Nevertheless, the sound they delivered can be customized in accordance with the demand of the performance. When it is played, the instrument is hung transversely in front of the chest or

• **朝鲜族长鼓舞表演**（图片提供：FOTOE）
Performance of the Korean Ethnic Tambourin Dance

朝鲜族长鼓
Tambourin of the Korean Ethnic Group

placed on a wood stand, with the left hand clapping on the tambourin while the right hand hits the tambourin with a bamboo plate. The Korean tambourin can produce a variety of rhythms to express lively or joyful emotions. It is mostly used in the traditional Korean tambourin dance of the Korean ethnic group. The dancer dances while playing it. It can also be used as the rhythm instrument in ensembles or accompanying music.

Elephant Foot Drum of the Ethnic Group of Dai

Elephant foot drum is a significant folk instrument for the Dai ethnic group. It acquired its name because of its resemblance to an elephant foot. Looking like a goblet, elephant foot drum is made out of a wood block, hollowed, with the upper goblet-shaped part serving as the resonator covered with skin tied down to the bottom part of the drum body by strips made of cow hide so as to adjust the tension of the skin. The outer surface of the drum is painted; the waist and

来定音。演奏时将鼓横挂胸前或放在木架上，左手拍鼓，右手执竹片敲击。长鼓能敲击出丰富多彩的节奏，常用来表现轻松、愉悦的情绪，多用在朝鲜族特有的长鼓舞中，由舞者边舞边击；亦可在合奏或伴奏中作为节奏乐器使用。

傣族象脚鼓

象脚鼓是傣族重要的民间乐器，其鼓身形似象脚，因而得名，其外形又与高脚杯相似。鼓身由

傣族象脚鼓
Elephant Foot Drum of the Ethnic Group of Dai

一整段木材制成，内体中空，上端是杯形共鸣体，鼓面蒙皮，鼓皮四周用细牛皮条勒紧，拴系于鼓腔下部，其松紧程度可自行调节。鼓身外表涂漆，鼓腰和鼓的下半部雕有装饰图案。鼓身上系黄色或其他颜色的绸带，傣族小伙将象脚鼓拷在肩上或斜挂在左胁下，双手击鼓，边敲边舞，鼓点复杂多变，舞者随鼓点踢腿、摆腰，激情狂舞，观众都为之沸腾喧嚣。

lower part are decorated with sculptured patterns. The drum body is tied with a satin band in yellow or other colors. The Dai youngsters put the elephant foot drum either on their shoulders or under the left arm and hit the drum with both hands while dancing. It has complicated and varied drumming points. The dancers caper to the drumming points with kicks and waist twists, dancing passionately and bringing a joyful atmosphere to all of the places within a hundred-mile radius.

• 傣族象脚鼓舞表演（图片提供：FOTOE）
Elephant Foot Drum Dance of the
Ethnic Group of Dai

一鼓作气

公元前684年的春天，强大的齐国出兵攻打鲁国。鲁庄公亲自率领军队前往应战，双方摆开阵势，准备大战一场。鲁国一位叫曹刿的将军率部队与齐国交战。当时，作战以擂鼓作为进攻号令，当齐军擂第一遍鼓时，曹刿按兵不动，齐军擂第二遍鼓时，曹刿还是没下令，齐军第三次准备进攻时，曹刿当机立断，对鲁庄公说："进攻的时机到了。"随着雨点般的战鼓声响起，鲁军将士奋勇出击，齐军被打得丢盔弃甲，四处溃逃。战斗胜利后，鲁庄公问曹刿："刚才为什么要等齐军擂了三次进军的鼓后，才出军？"曹刿说："打仗最重要的靠士气。擂第一遍鼓时，士气最旺；擂第二次鼓时，士兵的士气已经减退；擂第三次鼓时，士兵已经士气大减，情绪低落。这时我军再擂鼓进攻，用士气旺盛的军队去进攻松懈疲乏的军队，那当然能取胜啦！"这就是"一鼓作气"这个成语的来历，后来常用来比喻趁锐气旺盛之时鼓足干劲，一口气把事情做成。

Yi Gu Zuo Qi (Rousing the spirits with the first drum roll)

In the spring of 684 B.C., the powerful state of Qi launched its military forces against the state of Lu. Duke of Zhuang in Lu personally led his army to confront the invasion. Both sides were posed in formations and ready for a big fight. Lu has a military general, Cao Gui, who was commanding the army to fight against Qi. At that time, the military signals for charging were performed by drumming. When the Qi army gave out the first drum roll, Cao Gui didn't respond with his army. When the second roll came, Cao Gui still did not respond. When the Qi army gave out the third roll of drums, Cao made an immediate decision and told Duke of Zhuang, "It's time to charge." As the drumming rolled up like rumbling rain, the officers and men of Lu charged forward bravely and beat the Qi soldiers into dispersion in all directions. After the victory was claimed, Duke of Zhuang asked Cao Gui, "Why did you hold back our army from charging until the Qi army gave out the third roll of drumming?" Cao Gui replied, "The most important factor in the battle field is morale. The soldier's morale is at its highest point at the first drum roll; it decreases at the second roll, and eventually drops sharply at the third roll when most soldiers' spirits are at the lowest point. It was at this point that our first roll of charge will send out our soldiers in the highest morale to fight those tired and relaxed enemy soldiers. Of course, we will defeat them." That is the origin of the idiom, *Yi Gu Zuo Qi* (rousing the spirits with the first drum roll). It was later used to imply that one should take the initiative when one is in high spirits and full of preparations, to finish the job in one breath.

中国乐器大家族 The Extended Family of Chinese Musical Instruments

达卜

"达卜"是维吾尔语，一般译为"手鼓"。早在1400年前的南北朝时期，达卜就已出现，隋唐时期，达卜随着西域歌舞传入内地。长期以来，达卜广泛流传于民间，成为新疆维吾尔、乌兹别克、塔吉克和锡伯等少数民族的民间乐器。

达卜是在扁圆形的木制鼓框上，单面蒙以羊皮、小马皮或驴皮，现在多蒙以蟒皮，发音清脆响亮。在长期的发展中，各民族的达卜形制略有不同。维吾尔族达卜在框内周边缀有许多小铁环，击鼓时晃动作响。有大小两种：大达卜用于一般乐队和舞蹈伴奏，小达卜用于木卡姆乐队。塔吉克

Da Bu

Da Bu is a Uygur term, usually translated as "hand drum". *Da Bu* first appeared 1,400 years ago around the time of the Southern and Northern Dynasties (386-589). It was introduced to the Central Plains along with dance and music from the western regions in the Sui Dynasty (581-618) and Tang Dynasty (618-907). *Da Bu* has been popular in local societies ever since and has become the folk musical instrument among the ethnic minority groups of Uygur, Ozbek, Tajik and Xibe.

Da Bu is an oblate drum frame made of wood and covered with the skin of sheep, ponies or mules. It is now mostly covered with python skin for clear and crisp sounds. In the process of its long development, each ethnic group has come up with different shapes and forms. Uygur people adorn a lot of small iron rings around the inside of the frame so they will vibrate along with the drumming. There are two different *Da Bu*. The big *Da Bu* is used in common musical bands and dance accompaniment, while the small *Da Bu* serves the musical band for muqam performance. Tajik people's *Da Bu* is deeper though the

• **维吾尔族人打起手鼓唱起歌** (图片提供：FOTOE)
Uygur People Beating Hand Drum and Singing

族达卜鼓框略深，大小与维吾尔族大达卜近似，框内不缀铁环，有的装3对小钹，发音较低沉浑厚。这种鼓携带方便，甚至骑在马或骆驼上也可击奏。

达卜在演奏时以双手交替击鼓而发音。一般以右手击鼓心，发音"咚"，用于强音；左手击鼓边，发音"嗒"，用于弱音；双手击鼓边可作滚奏。其音色清脆响亮，声音力度变化幅度较大，演奏技巧灵活多变，可以起到烘托各种不同乐曲情节气氛的作用。

锣

锣是中国传统的打击乐器，应用范围极广，它用在民族乐队、民间器乐合奏、各种戏曲、曲艺以及歌舞伴奏中，在庆祝集会、赛龙舟、舞狮子、欢庆丰收和劳动竞赛中也是不可或缺的乐器。

锣是用铜制成，结构比较简单，锣身呈一个圆形的弧面，锣面中心通常有一块突起的圆形平面，称为"脐"，它对音色起着重要作用，有的锣脐呈半球形凸起，也有一些锣是无脐的平面锣。演奏者用

size is the same as Uygur people's big *Da Bu*. It doesn't have iron rings inside the frame, but has three pairs of small cymbals instead. It also sounds deeper and mellower. This kind of drum is easy and convenient to carry around and can be played on horseback or camelback.

When it is played, both hands alternately hit the drum for music. Usually, the right hand hits the center of the drum, which gives a "*dong*" sound for a strong tone, while the left hand hits the rim and gives a "*ta*" sound for a weak tone. Both hands can hit and roll at the same time. *Da Bu* is crisp and loud, with greater span for change in loudness. It also has flexible and changeable playing techniques and is able to play up the atmosphere for any kind of musical implication.

Gong

Gong (*Luo*) is a traditional Chinese percussion instrument and applied on a wide range of occasions. It is not only played in ethnic musical bands, folk instrument ensembles, various operas, vocal arts, and accompaniment performances, but also plays an indispensible part in festivals, gatherings, dragon boat racing, lion dancing, harvest

• 大锣
Big Gong

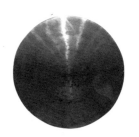

• 小锣
Small Gong

木槌敲击锣身正面的中央部分，产生振动而发音。

锣的历史悠久，最早使用铜锣的是居住在中国西南地区的少数民族。到了公元前2世纪左右，随着各民族文化交往的加强，铜锣逐渐向中国内地流传。那时，铜锣在战争中应用比较广泛。中国古代的军事术语"鸣金收兵"中的"金"就是古代铜锣的别称。

长期以来，由于应用的地区和场合的不同，锣的类型十分繁多，约有三十余种，其中常用的有大锣和小锣两种。

celebrations, and labor competitions.

Made of bronze in a simple structure, gong is basically a round and curved plate, usually with a small, bulged and round surface in the very center, called "navel", which is important to the timbre effect. In some cases, the gong may have the navel in a raised hemisphere, while in other cases, a gong may be just a plain surface without navel. The player uses a wood mallet to strike the center part of the gong for vibration and sounds.

The time-honored gong was first used by ethnic minority groups living in southwest China. In the 2nd century B.C., as cultural interaction progressed

大锣是铜锣类乐器当中体积最大的一种，直径在30~100厘米。它的特点是发音宏大，低沉而浑厚音色柔和，余音较长。在大型乐队中，大锣往往起到渲染气氛和增强节奏的作用，而在戏曲伴奏中则用以增强气氛和突出人物性格等。

小锣分为高音、中音和低音三

among ethnic groups, gong was gradually carried into the inland of China. At that time, gong was extensively used in wars. In the ancient Chinese military idiom, *Ming Jin Shou Bing* (striking the metal to signal retreat), *Jin* (metal) was an alias for ancient gong.

Since gong has long been used in different areas and on different occasions, there are approximately 30 or more different types of gong, among which the most common used are the big gong and small gong.

Big gong is the largest in the category of gong, with 30 to 100 centimeters in diameter. It is characterized by sonorous, deep, broad, and gentle tones as well as a prolonged lingering sound. In a large-scale band, big gong can work to heighten the atmosphere and enforce the rhythm. In the accompanying music for operas, it can be used to raise the atmosphere and highlight dramatic characters.

There are three kinds of small gong: the treble, the mediant and the bass. With the diameter running from 21 cm to 22.5 cm, small gong is a widely used accompanying instrument, especially in folk operas such as Beijing opera, Ping opera, *Bang Zi* opera and *Hua Gu* opera, vocal arts, drama, wind and percussion

• 敲锣铜女乐俑（明）
Figurine of Female Musician Playing Gong
(Ming Dynasty, 1368-1644)

种，直径在21厘米至22.5厘米之间，是一种用途广泛的伴奏乐器，尤其是在京剧、评剧、梆子戏、花鼓戏等地方戏曲，以及曲艺、话剧、吹打乐队和民间舞蹈中广泛使用。

除了大锣和小锣之外，还有一种由若干大小相同而厚度、音高存在区别的小锣组合而成的云锣。这些小锣以次序悬挂于木架上，每一个小锣都由三根绳吊在木架的方框中。云锣的演奏方法与小锣类似，用小槌击奏，其常见编制为十个一组，也有十四个一组和二十四个一组的大型云锣。云锣音色清澈、圆润、悦耳，余音持久，但音量不大，常在各类乐队中起到点缀的作用。

band and folk dances.

In addition to big gong and small gong, there is another kind of gong made up of several small gongs with the same size but different thickness and treble, called cloud gong (*Yun Luo*). These small gongs are arranged according to the order of their sound and hung on a wood rack, each of them being tied by three robes onto the square frame of the rack. The playing method of cloud gong is the same as that of small gong, being beaten by a small hammer. The common form of cloud gong is 10, 14, or even 24 small gongs in a set. It has clear and penetrating sounds, pleasantly full and mellow, with long-lasting lingering sounds. Since it doesn't have a loud volume, it usually serves ornamental roles in various musical bands.

一锤定音

锣的结构虽然简单，制作工艺却并不简单，有熔炼、浇铸、锻片、淬火、刮削、调音等多道工序。从前乐器作坊所制的锣在卖出前都没有"音"，打击时只能发出闷响。买主必须说清锣的用处和需要的音调及响度，由经验丰富的老师傅根据买主的要求用轻敲的方法在锣上选好适当部位，然后拿捏好力度猛打一锤；提起锣再打，就会发出符合需要的悦耳、响亮的声音，而且不易变调。这道手续叫"开锣"。因为老师傅这一锤与音色优劣有密切关系，所以"一锤定音"便成了制锣作坊的专用语。沿用到后来，这个成语就比喻凭某个人的一句话作出决定。

Yi Chui Ding Yin (One Strike Determines the Sound)

In spite of its simple structure, the manufacture of gong is not a simple job, for it involves such laborious working processes as smelting, casting, forging, quenching, shaving and tuning. In the past, all the manufactured gongs from instrument factories were "voiceless" before they were sold. When one hit the drum, it would just give a muffled sound. The customer should prescribe the usage, the tone and the volume, and the experienced craftsman would try knocking lightly on the gong in order to locate the right spot in accordance with the customer's requirements. The craftsman then exerted modulated strength and gave it a master strike; the next minute, one would hear him beating the raised gong, producing the loud and pleasant sounds in compliance with the demands. The tune was not easy to go away. This procedure is called "open gong". Since the craftsman's master strike has much to do with the determination of the quality of the instrument, Yi Chui Ding Yin has become a lingo in the industry of Luo manufacturing. It is still used to imply that things are decided by someone's final words.

钹

钹是一种在中国各地广为流传的铜制打击乐器，古代称"铜钹"、"铜盘"，而在民间称"镲"。钹的构造简单，钹体为一圆形铜板，中部隆起的半球形部分称为"碗"或"帽"，碗与钹边之间的部分叫"堂"，碗的顶

Cymbal

Cymbal (Bo) is a very common percussion instrument made of copper across China. In ancient times, it was called "copper cymbal", or "copper plate", while in local societies, it was called Cha. Cymbal is structurally simple: a body of a round copper plate with the center part bulged up like a half ball, called "bowl" or "hat". Between the bowl and the rim of cymbal is the area called Tang. There is a small hole at the top of

• 击钹伎乐俑（唐）
Figurine of a Musician Beating a
Cymbal (Tang Dynasty, 618-907)

部钻有小孔，用绸或布拴系。演奏者常取站姿，双手各持一枚，通过钹巾持住钹身，相对合击后振动发音。也可以将钹悬挂在支架上，用鼓槌滚奏，表现力极强。

钹发音清脆，铿锵有力，常用于京剧、地方戏和民间歌舞的伴奏，并且是民间喜庆锣鼓"四大件"（鼓、大锣、小锣、钹）之一。

the bowl, where a piece of cloth or satin is tied. The performer stands to play the cymbal, with each hand holding a cymbal through the tightly knotted cloth, and clapping both cymbals against each other to produce sounds. It can also be hung on a rack and rolled with a drum stick for rich expressiveness.

Cymbal has crisp and powerful sounds. It is often used for accompanying music in Beijing opera, local operas and folk dance, and is claimed to be one of the "Four Major Pieces", drum, big gong, small gong, cymbal, in local celebrations.

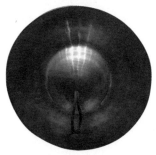

• 作为京剧伴奏乐器的铜钹
　Copper Cymbal Used as Accompanying
　Instrument in Beijing Opera

• 铜钹（金）
　Copper Cymbal (Jin Dynasty,
　1115-1234)

梆子

梆子又名"梆板"，是一种木制打击乐器，约在明末清初随着梆子腔戏曲的兴起而流行。根据流行的地域不同，梆子有河北梆子、南梆子、坠梆和秦梆之分。

河北梆子流行于河北、河南、山东一带，用于梆子戏曲和民间器乐合奏。多用紫檀木、红木或枣木制作。两根长短、粗细不同的硬木棒，细长的一根为圆柱形，短粗的一根为长方形，以左手执长方形木棒，右手执圆形木棒，相交成十字形，互击发声，音色清脆、坚实。

南梆子又称"广东板"，广泛流行于南方地区，发音短促、圆润，在戏曲和民间器乐合奏中使用，也用于京剧高拨子唱腔的伴

• 河北梆子
Hebei Wooden Stick

Wooden Stick

Wooden stick (*Bang Zi*), also known as Bang Ban, is a percussion instrument made of wood. It became popular with the rise of the opera of *Bang Zi* tone around the end of the Ming Dynasty (1368-1644) and the beginning of the Qing Dynasty (1644-1911). Based on the regions of its popularity, it is classified into Hebei wooden stick, south wooden stick, *Zhui* wooden stick and *Qin* wooden stick.

Hebei wooden stick prevails in the areas of Hebei, Henan and Shandong provinces, and is applied in the opera of *Bang Zi* and the ensemble of folk instruments. It is mostly made of rosewood, redwood or jujube wood. It composes of a pair of hardwood clubs of different sizes and lengths. The longer and thinner one is round, held in the right hand, while the shorter and thicker one is square, held in the left hand. Both are posed in a cross and struck against each other to produce clear, crisp and solid sounds.

South wooden stick, also known as Guangdong *Ban*, was popularized in the southern area. It has short but mellow sounds and is used in operas

中国乐器大家族

The Extended Family of Chinese Musical Instruments

• 南梆子
South Wooden Stick

奏。南梆子多以花梨木制作，为长方形中空体，中间有一个长方形音孔。演奏时以左手执梆，右手执一竹签或木槌敲击。

坠梆又称"脚踏梆子"，用于豫剧及河南坠子的伴奏。其外形如鸭蛋，梆与槌连为一体。演奏时常绑于桌腿上，用脚控制木槌击梆发音。演奏者常由演奏坠琴的演员兼任。

秦梆多用来给秦腔伴奏，为椭圆形木制，长约20厘米。

木鱼

木鱼最早是佛教的一种法器，随着佛教传入中国，在寺院中一直

or folk instrument ensembles, or in accompaniment to the singing tune of *Gao Ba Zi* in Beijing opera. South wooden stick is mostly made of a rosewood block, hollowed in a rectangular shape with a rectangular sound hole in the middle. It is held in the left hand while the right hand uses a bamboo stick or wood mallet to strike against it.

Zhui wooden stick, also called "pedle wooden stick", is used as an accompanying instrument for Yu opera and Henan *Zhui Zi*. It looks like a duck egg, with the stick and the hammer connected with each other. It is usually tied to a leg of a table and a foot is used to control the wood hammer and strike the stick. It is usually played by the

用于聚集僧众和诵经之中，也用于佛教音乐"梵呗"的伴奏，带有浓厚的宗教色彩。明代以后，木鱼逐渐流行于民间，用于说唱木鱼歌和昆曲的伴奏，后来又逐渐在歌舞伴奏和器乐合奏中应用。目前，木鱼除在佛教、道教音乐中使用外，还广泛用于各种形式的器乐合奏和乐队中。在民族乐队中，备有音高不同、数量不等的成套木鱼，常用于轻快活泼的乐曲中，有时可独奏简短的乐句，或用来模仿马蹄声的音响效果，十分逼真。

木鱼用木料雕刻而成，形制有长鱼形和团鱼形两种，二者规格不一，用途也各不相同。

• 团鱼形木鱼
Round-fish Wooden Knocker

same *Zhui Qin* (two-stringed zither with fingerboard) performer.

Qin wooden stick is used to accompany *Qin Qiang*. It is made of wood in an oval shape, about 20 centimeters long.

Wooden Knocker

Wooden knocker (*Mu Yu*) was at first a Buddhist item, imported to China along with Buddhism, and has been used to assemble monks or recite sutras in monasteries. It has also been used in accompaniment with the Buddhist music of Fan Bei with strong religious flavors. After the Ming Dynasty (1368-1644), wooden koncker became gradually popular in local societies to accompany the performance of the wooden koncker song storytelling and *Kun Qu* opera. It was later gradually applied in accompaniment with singing and dancing, and in instrument ensembles as well. In addition to its current usage in Buddhist and Taoist music, wooden knocker is extensively used in various forms of instrument ensembles and musical bands. In a ethnic musical band, complete sets of wooden knocker prepared with various pitches and in different numbers are often used for relaxed and lively music.

● 北京法源寺里的长鱼形木鱼（图片提供：FOTOE）
The Long-fish Wooden Knocker in Beijing Fayuan Temple

　　长鱼形木鱼又称"梆木鱼"，外形雕刻成长鱼形状，有口有眼，通体饰以鱼鳞、云纹等图案。一般体长100～150厘米、高25～40厘米。这种木鱼多使用桑木或椿木制作，为古代大型佛教寺院所专用，常用铁索吊挂于佛殿前，用于僧众聚集或斋饭时敲击。木槌用圆木棒制作。广东音乐的乐队常用长鱼形木鱼，通常使用大小两个木鱼，大

Sometimes it can be performed in a brief, solo phrase, or in picturesque mimicry of hoofbeat of horses.

Wooden knocker is carved out of a woodblock. Based on the shapes, there are long fish type and round fish type. They are made with different specifications and used for different purposes.

The long fish type of wooden knocker, also called *Bang* wooden knocker, is carved into the shape of a long fish with a mouth and eyes, and the entire body is covered with patterns of scales and clouds. Generally, the long-fish wooden knocker measures 100 cm to 150 cm long, and is 25 cm to 40 cm tall. They are mostly made of mulberry wood or mahogany and were exclusively used in the large Buddhist temples in ancient times, hung on iron cables in front of the Buddhist hall and sounded for monk gatherings or meals. The wood hammer is in the shape of a round wood log. The musical bands of Guangdong often make use of long-fish wooden knocker, a big one and a small one, with the big one for bass and the small one for treble.

The round-fish wooden knocker, also called Song wooden knocker, is carved into a hollowed fish head with a

木鱼发低音，小木鱼发高音。

团鱼形木鱼又称"诵木鱼"，外形雕刻成鱼头状，腹部中空，头部正前方横开一个长条形"鱼口"以出音，尾部盘绕，背部（即敲击部位）呈斜坡形，有的小木鱼在尾部还有短小的握柄。外表雕刻有各种鱼纹图案，糅红色漆描金花纹。这种木鱼规格较多，大木鱼圆径40厘米左右，小木鱼圆径7厘米左右。演奏时，大团鱼形木鱼需置于地面上，小团鱼形木鱼则用左手托持，右手执木槌敲击。这种木鱼发音短促，音色清脆洪亮，是富有特色的节奏乐器，常用在戏剧、曲艺伴奏、器乐合奏、民族乐队和宗教音乐中。

long open gap, the "fish mouth", running horizontally through the front to utter sounds. The tail coils and the back (that is, the area to be knocked at) slants. In some cases, the small wooden knocker may have a short handle at the tail. The surface is decorated with different fish patterns and lacquered in red color with golden lines. This kind of wooden knocker has a variety of specifications. The big one may have 40 centimeters or so for the circular diameter, while the small one might be around 7 centimeters. When it is played, the big round-fish wooden knocker is supposed to be placed on the ground and the small one can be held in the left hand, with the right hand using a wooden hammer to knock at it. This kind of wooden knocker is featured by its short, but crisp and sonorous sound. It is a rhythm instrument with special characteristics, often used in drama, accompanying music for vocal arts, instrumental ensembles, ethnic bands and religious music.

• 云南大理白族雕花木鱼
Sculptured Wooden Knocker of the Ethnic Group of Bai, Dali, Yunnan Province

玄奘大师与木鱼

玄奘是中国唐代的高僧，曾跋涉万里到天竺（今印度）取经，为中国佛教的发展和中外文化交流做出了巨大的贡献。传说他从天竺归来的途中偶遇一位长者。这位长者早年丧妻，留下个只有三岁的儿子。后来他又续娶了一个女子，这个后母十分厌恶孩子，趁长者出猎时从楼上将孩子扔进了河里。长者为了超度儿子，常常为路过的僧人提供斋饭。玄奘大师入席之后，告诉长者："我长途跋涉，非常疲劳，希望能吃点鱼肉。"在场的人听了都很惊讶。长者起身要出去买鱼，玄奘又嘱咐他："一定要大鱼才好。"长者于是买回一条大鱼，才割开鱼腹，就见到自己的孩子在鱼腹中啼哭。长者惊喜交集。玄奘大师说："这孩子前世积德，所以现今虽被鱼吞，却得不死。"长者问："如何报答鱼恩？"玄奘大师告诉他："以木雕成鱼形，悬于佛寺，斋时敲击，可以报鱼德。"传说这就是佛寺中木鱼的来历。

Master Xuanzang and Wooden Knocker

Xuanzang was an eminent Chinese monk in the Tang Dynasty (618-907). His long and difficult trip to the faraway Tianzhu (ancient India) for the acquisition of Buddhist sutras has immensely conduced to the development of Chinese Buddhism as well as the cultural interchange between China and foreign countries. It was said that on his back trip, he met with a senior, whose wife had gone away when they were still young and left him a three-year-old son. Later, he married another woman, but the stepmother hated this son. She took the chance when the husband was out hunting, and threw the child to the river to be drowned. In order to memorialize his son, the old man often offered meals to the monks passing by. After Xuanzang entered for the meal, he told the old man, "I have traveled far and got exhausted. I hope I can have some fish meat." All the people present were stunned at hearing this. The old man rose and was ready to go out and buy a fish when Xuanzang added, "It should be a big fish." Therefore, the old man brought a big fish. As he cut open the fish belly, he saw his child crying in the belly of the fish. The old man felt as surprised as happy. Xuanzang told the old man, "This child accumulated a lot of good karma in his previous life, that's why he didn't die after being swallowed by the fish." The old man asked, "How should I repay the fish?" Xuanzang replied to him, "Carve a fish out of a wood block and hang it in front of the Buddhist temple. Knocking on the wooden fish at meal time is a repayment to the fish." That's how the wooden knocker came into being.

● 玄奘法师像
Portrait of Master Xuanzang

拍板

拍板简称"板"，古时多用檀木制作，又名"檀板"。又因唐代玄宗年间，梨园乐工黄幡绰善奏此板，故又称"绰板"。

古代拍板由西北少数民族地区传入中原，唐代已广为流传，但只

Clapper

Clapper (*Pai Ban*) is sometimes called *Ban* for short. It is made of ebony, so it is also known as ebony *Ban*. It was played by a noted opera musician, Huang FanChuo, in the reign of Emperor Xuanzong in the Tang Dynasty (618-907), and is therefore called *Chuo Ban* as well.

Clapper was introduced to the Central Plains in ancient times from the ethnic minority groups in the northwestern areas. In the Tang Dynasty (618-907), it had become prevalent, but only used in *San* music, a kind of popular music in local societies. It varied in size, with the big clapper composed of 9 pieces of plates and the small one composed of 6 pieces. On the murals in the Muogao Grottoes of Dunhuang, images of clapper musicians were present. According the stone sculptures of music and dance, unearthed from the tomb of the Five Dynasties (907-960), it was learned that clapper was already an important rhythm instrument in the court musical bands at that time. In the Song

• 奏拍板者砖雕（五代）
Brick Sculpture of Clapper Player (Five Dynasties, 907-960)

• 顾闳中《韩熙载夜宴图》（五代）（局部）

Han Xizai's Night Banquet by Gu Hongzhong (Five Dynasties, 907-960) (partial)

在民间流行的"散乐"中使用。有大小之分，大的九块板，小的六块板。在敦煌千佛洞的唐代壁画中，绘有打拍板的乐伎形象。从五代时期墓葬的乐舞石刻还可以看出，在当时的宫廷乐队中，拍板已是重要的节奏乐器。宋代，拍板在民间说唱中普遍应用。到了元代，拍板用于宫廷宴乐，也是杂剧的伴奏乐器。明清时期的宫廷音乐都使用拍，并且广泛用于民间器乐合奏和

Dynasty (960-1279), clapper was widely applied in the folk art of storytelling. In the Yuan Dynasty (1206-1368), it was used in imperial banquets as well as accompanying music for *Za* opera (a form of Chinese opera). Both the Ming Dynasty (1368-1644) and Qing Dynasty (1644-1911) used clapper in their court music. It was widely used in folk instrument ensembles as well as the accompanying music for folk operas.

Modern clapper is composed of three

• 京剧伴奏所用的云板
Yun Clapper in Accompaniment with Beijing Opera

地方戏曲的伴奏。

　　现代拍板多以三块长方形紫檀木、红木或黄杨木板组成，长18～20厘米，宽4～6厘米。前两块板用丝弦缠绕，然后用布带与后面的单块木板连接。演奏时以左手执后板，撞击前两块木板发声。拍板常与板鼓合用，由鼓手兼操。

rectangular pieces of rosewood, redwood, or boxwood, measuring 18 to 20 centimeters long and 4 to 6 centimeters wide. The first two pieces are tied with silk strings and connected with the third single piece with cloth bands. When it is played, the left hand holds the last piece of board and knocks it against the first two pieces to produce sounds. Clapper is often used in combination with *Ban* drum, both being played by the drummer.

张翀《瑶池仙聚图》（明）

这件作品描写的是八仙聚乐于瑶池的场景，其中曹国舅手中所持的宝物就是拍板。

Fairy Gathering at Yaochi by Zhang Chong
(Ming Dynasty, 1368-1644)

This work of art depicts the scene where the Eight Immortals gathered together around Yaochi. One of the immortals, Cao Guojiu, held in his hand a clapper.

乐器合奏与乐队
Instrument Ensembles and Musical Bands

　　除了各种乐器的独奏之外，中国民族器乐还包括各种不同乐器组合的重奏与合奏。纯粹用锣鼓等打击乐器合奏的清锣鼓乐，音色丰富，节奏性强，擅长表现热烈、活泼的生活情趣。吹管乐器与弦乐器合奏的丝竹乐，风格细致，多表现轻快活泼的情绪。而吹管乐器和打击乐器合奏的吹打乐，风格粗犷，擅长表现热烈欢快的情绪。

In addition to various instrument solos, Chinese ethnic instruments are also played in ensembles and orchestra performances. The ensemble based solely on percussion instruments such as gong and drum, is featured by rich tones and strong beats with skillful expressiveness for the fervent and lively fun in life. The combination of pipe wind instruments and string instruments in silk and bamboo music displays a refined style capable of smooth, light and delightful sentiments, while the combination of pipe wind instruments and percussion instruments in wind and percussion music is characterized by a straightforward and unrestrained style with skillful expressiveness of fervent and joyful atmosphere.

> 丝竹乐

丝竹乐主要流行在中国南方各地，是一种丝弦乐器与竹管乐器合奏的音乐形式。最古老的丝竹演奏以琴瑟与箫管组成，常为歌唱或舞蹈伴奏，后来发展为独立的演奏形式，常在饮宴中用以助兴。丝竹乐风格轻快活泼，演奏精致细腻，具有优美秀雅、柔和清澈的音乐性格，在中国南方较为盛行。

江南丝竹

中国传统器乐丝竹乐的一种，流行于江苏南部和浙江一带。明代嘉靖年间，以魏良辅为首的戏曲音乐家组成了规模完整的丝竹乐队，后逐渐形成丝竹演奏的专职班社。明万历末年在吴中（苏州地区）形成了新的乐种"弦索"，它与民俗活动密切结合，后正式定名为"江

> Silk and Bamboo Music

Silk and bamboo (*Si Zhu*) music prevails in the southern places of China. It is a musical combination form of silk string instruments and bamboo windpipe instruments. The oldest performance of silk and bamboo music was done by 7-stringed zither (*Qin*), 50-stringed zither with movable bridges (*Se*), and vertical flute (*Xiao*), often served to accompany singing or dancing. It later developed into an individual form of performance and served as background music in banquets for a joyful atmosphere. Silk and bamboo music has a delightful and lively style with sophisticated and delicate performance methods and graceful, gentle, and translucent musical characteristics. It is more popular in south China.

Jiangnan Silk and Bamboo

As a kind of the Chinese traditional instrument music of silk and bamboo,

• 上海城隍庙湖心亭（用片提供：FOTOE）
Huxin Pavilion of Town's God Temple in Shanghai

南丝竹"。20世纪初，上海的江南丝竹演奏活动最有影响，当时一批丝竹乐爱好者经常在上海城隍庙湖心亭搞活动，演奏技艺越来越精细，乐曲也逐步得到丰富和提高。

江南丝竹的乐队特色鲜明，灵便多样，一般少则三、四人，多则十人左右，常用笛、箫、笙、二胡、琵琶、小三弦、扬琴、板、荸荠鼓等乐器。江南丝竹音乐的最大特点之一，就是演奏风格精细，

Jiangnan silk and bamboo is prevalent in south Jiangsu and Zhejiang areas. During the Jiajing Period in the Ming Dynasty (1368-1644), a group of operatic musicians, headed by Wei Liangfu, organized a complete musical band of silk and bamboo, which later grew gradually into a professional troupe of silk and bamboo performance. At the end of the Wanli Period (1573-1620) in the Ming Dynasty, a new kind of musical, Xian Suo, emerged in the Wuzhong (Suzhou areas) and became closely tied to folk events. It was later formally named "Jiangnan silk and bamboo". At the beginning of the 20th century, the performance of Jiangnan silk and bamboo in Shanghai became the most influential activity when groups of silk and bamboo music enthusiasts gathered together and held frequent events at the Huxin Pavilion of the town's god temple in Shanghai. The playing skills became more and more refined, and the musical pieces also grew more plentiful and advanced.

The musical band of Jiangnan silk and bamboo has distinctive styles, nimble and diversified, composed of three or four people in a small band, or 10 people in a large one. It usually includes such musical instruments as

● 江南丝竹乐队瓷像
Porcelain Statues of Jiangnan Silk and Bamboo Band

各个乐器声部既富有个性又互相和谐。也有人将江南丝竹的特点概括为"花、细、轻、小、活"五个字，即华彩、细腻、轻松、小巧和灵活。江南丝竹的乐曲多来自于民间婚丧喜庆和庙会活动的风俗音乐，还有的是长期流传于民间的古典曲牌。其中最著名的八首乐曲，称为"八大曲"，包括《欢乐歌》、《三六》、《云庆》、《中花六板》、《行街》、《慢三六》、《慢六板》、《四合如意》。

广东音乐

广东音乐是中国丝竹乐的一种，流行于珠江三角洲一带。清末民初时，广东戏曲的伴奏乐队和街头艺人常演奏戏曲中的过场音乐和民间小曲，这些音乐被当地人称为"过场"、"小曲"等。以后逐渐形成富有当地特色的音乐类型，并且传往外地，人称"广东音乐"。

19世纪下半叶，广东音乐在广州地区流行时，其乐队以琵琶为主奏乐器，另有筝、箫、三弦、椰胡等。20世纪20年代以前，广东音乐使用俗称为"五架头"的乐队组合，即二弦（粗弦硬弓的拉弦乐

flute, vertical flute, *Sheng*, *Er Hu*, pear-shaped lute, small three-strings, dulcimer, clapper, and *Bi Qi* drum (*Ban* drum). The most striking feature of Jiangnan silk and bamboo music is the delicacy of its performance style, with the sounds from each individual instrument being so distinctive and mutually harmonious at the same time. Some people conclude the features of Jiangnan silk and bamboo in five Chinese characters: *Hua*, *Xi*, *Qing*, *Xiao*, and *Huo*, namely, gorgeous, delicate, relaxed, compact, and nimble in plain words. Most of the musical pieces of Jiangnan silk and bamboo come from folk music from weddings, funerals, celebrations, and festivals in the local societies. There are also some classic *Qu Pai* (a generic term for a fixed melody used in traditional Chinese music) that have been passed down through generations in the local societies, the most famous among which are the eight great musical pieces called "eight melodies (*Ba Da Qu*)": *Huan Le Ge*, *San Liu*, *Yun Qing*, *Zhong Hua Liu Ban*, *Xing Jie*, *Man San Liu*, *Man Liu Ban*, and *Si He Ru Yi*.

Guangdong Music

Guangdong music is a kind of Chinese silk and bamboo music, prevailing in

● 广彩仕女婴戏乐舞图盘（清）
Guangdong-enameled Plate with Picture of
Maid and Child Playing Music and Dancing
(Qing Dynasty, 1644-1911)

器）、提琴（类似板胡）、三弦、
月琴、横箫五种乐器。20年代中
期，改以粤胡和扬琴为主奏乐器，
其他乐器有秦琴、椰胡、洞箫等，
称为"软弓组合"。之后，广东音
乐的乐队又增加了许多丝竹乐器。

广东音乐音色清脆明亮，旋律
流畅优美，节奏活泼欢快。乐曲结
构多为短小单一的小品，很少有大
型套曲，尤其擅长于对生活小境的
描摹，对传统的生活情趣无不流露
着关注，因浓郁的地方色彩而具有
独特的艺术魅力。

the region of the Pearl River Delta. In
the late Qing Dynasty (1644-1911) to
the Republican Period (1912-1949), the
accompanying band of operas and street
performers always performed interludes
and folk ditties, respectively called *Guo
Chang* and *Xiao Qu*. They later grew to
be a typical category of local music and
were exported to other places, henceforth
called "Guangdong music".

In the second half of the 19th century,
when Guangdong music became popular
in the Guangzhou areas, the musical band
was based on the key instrument of the
pear-shaped lute, supported by *Zheng*,

• 徐渭《蕉石图》（明）

《雨打芭蕉》是广东音乐中早期的经典曲目之一，乐谱最初见于1917年。全曲旋律流畅明快，一连串乐符犹如淅淅沥沥的雨点敲打着芭蕉，使人联想到芭蕉婆娑起舞之态，表达了一种喜悦之情。乐曲所表现的意境极富南国风情。

Picture of Chinese Banana Tree and Rock by Xu Wei (Ming Dynasty, 1368-1644)

Raindrops Beating Chinese Banana Tree Leaves is a classic piece in the early period of Guangdong music. Its musical notation first appeared 1917. The overall rhythm runs in smooth and fluent flow with series of short phrases of small, light beats in mimicry of the raindrops falling on the banana leaves, which reminds people of the whirling dance of banana leaves as well as a sense of joy. The melody is highly flavored with the spirit of the southern China.

vertical flute, three-strings, *Ye Hu* and others. Before the 1920s, Guangdong music took the forms of the so-called *Wu Jia Tou* band formation, made up of the five instruments of two-strings (a plucked string instrument with thick strings and hard arrows), *Ti Qin* (something like *Ban Hu*), three-strings, *Yue Qin*, and transverse *Xiao*. During the mid-twenties, the key instruments were replaced by *Yue Hu* and dulcimer, and supplemented with such instruments as *Qin Qin, Ye Hu* and vertical flute. The whole formation is called "soft-arrow combination" (*Ruan Gong Zu He*). Later, the band of Guangdong music added the instruments of silk and bamboo.

Guangdong music is featured by a crisp and bright tone, fluent and graceful melody, as well as lively and joyful rhythms. The musical pieces, mostly short and single and rarely large-scaled in suites, are particularly good at expressing those insignificant scenes in life with revealed concerns about the fun of the traditional way of life. Its artistic attrition is built exactly on the dense local flavors.

福建南音

　　福建南音又称"南曲"、"南乐"、"南管"等，是流行于福建南部的晋江、龙溪和厦门等地的丝竹乐，在中国的台湾、香港等地区及南洋群岛（菲律宾、新加坡、马来西亚、印度尼西亚等地）华侨旅居的地区也很盛行。

　　南音所用的乐器主要有洞箫、琵琶、二弦、三弦、拍板等。其中，洞箫共九节、长约59厘米，与唐代的竹制管乐器"尺八"规格一致；所用的琵琶、拍板等也与建于唐代的泉州开元寺拱梁上飞天女伎手捧的乐器相似；而福建南音乐队中弹奏琵琶至今仍沿用唐、五代时期的习惯，采取横抱姿势弹奏。再加上福建南音中的诸多曲名，多见于汉、唐时期的文献，所以福建南音又有"唐宋遗音"之称，被人称为音乐文化的"活化石"。

　　在漫长的历史进程中，福建南音由宫廷走向民间，形成了一种个性独特、雅俗共赏的传统音乐，古朴、典雅、舒缓、低回的音调，常常用以抒发哀怨、忧伤、深情、思念等情绪，极富感染力。

Fujian *Nan Yin*

Fujian *Nan Yin*, also known as *Nan Qu, Nan Yue, Nan Guan*, and the like, is a kind of silk and bamboo music which prevails in such places as Jinjiang, Longxi, and Xiamen in the south of Fujian Province. It's also popular in Taiwan and Hong Kong of China, and the South Pacific Islands (Philippines, Singapore, Malaysia, Indonesia, and so on) areas where overseas Chinese inhabit.

　　The main instruments of *Nan Yin* include vertical flute, pear-shaped lute, two-strings, three-strings, clapper, and so on. Among them, the vertical flute is a 9-section bamboo pipe around 59 centimeters long, with the same specifications with the bamboo pipe instrument *Chi Ba* in the Tang Dynasty (618-907); the pear-shaped lute and clapper are similar to those held by the flying female musicians portrayed on the arched beam at the Kaiyuan Temple in Quanzhou established in the Tang Dynasty. Besides, the performance of pear-shaped lute in Fujian *Nan Yin* bands retains the convention handed down from the Tang Dynasty and the Five Dynasties (907-960), which places the instrument in transverse position for playing. On top of that, many titles of the *Nan Yin* musical

● 福建南音表演（图片提供：CFP）
Performance of Fujian *Nan Yin*

潮州弦诗

　　潮州弦诗是流行于广东省潮州、汕头一带的传统丝竹乐。"弦诗乐"原指以潮州民间的丝弦、弹拨乐器演奏古诗谱，现在已经逐渐成为潮州民间丝弦、吹管、弹拨等乐器独奏、重奏、合奏等演奏形式的总称。流行地域除了广东省东南的潮汕地区之外，在福建南部以及东

pieces are recorded in those literature of the Han Dynasty (206 B.C.- 220 A.D.) and Tang Dynasty. All these make Fujian *Nan Yin* deserve the title of "Legacy sounds of Tang and Song dynasties" (*Tang Song Yi Yin*). It is praised as the "living fossil" of the musical culture.

During its long process of historical development, Fujian *Nan Yin* has made its way from the court to the local society, and formed a traditional music with strong character and universal appeal.

南亚的泰国、越南、马来西亚等地均有流传。

潮州弦诗可分为"儒家乐"和"棚顶乐"两种。其中"儒家乐"的演奏者一种是由上层社会资助的乐队，另一种则是自发性的群众自由集社组织，演奏风格纤细、雅致，重神韵，多用于民间婚丧喜庆等场合。"棚顶乐"则主要用于戏曲舞台，风格简朴、粗犷。目前民间流传的弦诗乐，多属于"儒家乐"。

潮州弦诗最早只以七弦琴演

• 月琴
Yue Qin

Its primitive, unsophisticated, elegant, relaxed and resonating tunes are often used to express the affecting emotions of complaining sadness, sorrow, sentiment and yearning.

Chaozhou *Xian Shi*

Chaozhou *Xian Shi* is a traditional silk and bamboo music popular in Chaozhou and Shantou of Guangdong Province. *Xian Shi* music was originally a local performance in Chaozhou with silk string and plucked string instruments played for classic poetry. It has become a general term for the local performance of silk string, plucked string, and wind instruments in solos, ensembles or instrument ensembles in Chaozhou. In addition to the Chaozhou and Shantou areas in the southeastern part of Guangdong, it is also popularized in the southeastern Asian areas like Thailand, Vietnam and Malaysia.

There are two kinds of Chaozhou *Xian Shi*: "Confucianist music" and "tent-top music". Some of the musical bands of Confucianist music are sponsored by the upper class of the society, while others are organized by voluntary crowds as free communities. Their performance is

奏，之后以竹弦、洞箫、月琴三种乐器组成小型的丝竹乐队。18世纪以来，又吸收了多种乐器。潮州弦诗总的特点是旋律由繁到简，速度由慢而快，在高潮中结束全曲。尤其引人入胜的是其往往通过旋律音高的微妙变化，产生特殊艺术效果，赋予乐曲以特殊的韵味和情趣。

characterized by a refined and elegant style with stress placed on its artistic charm. The occasions are mostly local weddings, funerals, celebrations and festivals. "Tent-top music" is mostly used on the stage for dramas or opera, with a plain and unsophisticated style. The prevalent *Xian Shi* music in the local society presently belongs to "Confucianist music".

Originally, Chaozhou *Xian Shi* was played solely by 7-stringed zither; later, another three instruments, bamboo strings (*Zhu Xian*), vertical flute, and *Yue Qin*, joined in and formed a small-scale silk and bamboo band. Since the 18th century, it has recruited many other instruments. On the whole, the typical feature of Chaozhou *Xian Shi* lies in the shift of the rhythm from the complicated to the simplified, its speed from slow to fast, with all of the music ending with a climax. An intriguing aspect is its special artistic effects produced through the minute change in the pitch of the rhythm, endowing the piece with special charm and fun.

> 吹打乐

吹打乐就是由吹管乐器和打击乐器结合起来演奏的音乐形式,民间俗称"锣鼓"或"鼓吹"。吹打乐在中国民间广泛流传,主要演奏场合为庆典、节日、婚丧和农闲季节的迎神赛会等,其特点是乐队人数众多,常演奏长篇大套的乐曲,风格热烈而粗犷。

> Wind and Percussion Music

Wind and percussion music (*Chui Da* music) is a musical form which combines wind instruments and percussion instruments, and is commonly referred to as *Luo Gu* or *Gu Chui* in local societies. Wind and percussion music has been prevalent in Chinese society, mostly during celebrations, festivals, weddings, funerals and temple festivals between farming seasons. It is characterized by big groups of band members and large-scaled musical suites with heated and unrestrained styles.

● "骑马鼓吹"模印砖画(南朝)
Printed Brick Painting of *Horseback Gu Chui* (South Dynasty, 420-589)

浙东锣鼓

浙东锣鼓又称"浙东吹打"，流行于浙江省东部的嵊县、宁波、奉化、舟山等地，盛行于明代中叶。旧时多用于婚丧、喜庆等活动。据说，明朝戚继光征平倭寇，各地艺人汇集沿海迎接军队凯旋，其中就有浙东锣鼓的演出。此外每年举行的"迎会"都有浙东锣鼓参演。它的曲调来源于民歌和本省的戏曲音乐。乐队编制各地不尽相同，常用的乐器有吹管乐、丝弦乐和打击乐三种，最有特色的要数锣鼓乐器，演奏技巧极其复杂。

Zhedong *Luo Gu*

Zhedong *Luo Gu*, also known as "Zhedong wind and percussion music", prevails in several areas in the cast of Zhejiang Province such as Shengxian, Ningbo, Fenghua, and Zhoushan among others. It had already been popular in the mid-Ming Dynasty (1368-1644). It used to be performed at weddings, funerals, celebrations, and other occasions. It is reported that the music was played during the Ming Dynasty when General Qi Jiguang and his army defeated the Japanese pirates and were welcomed by all the performers on the coasts. It is also

● 浙东锣鼓表演
Performance of Zhedong *Luo Gu*

戚继光平倭

戚继光(1528—1587)，明代著名将领、军事家。日本在中国古代被称为"倭"，来自日本的海盗因此被称为"倭寇"。戚继光出生于明朝中叶嘉靖年间，当时东南沿海的倭寇之患十分严重，日本海盗经常四处抢掠，而明朝军队腐败，常吃败仗。嘉靖三十四年（1555年），戚继光被调往浙江，招募新军，并于1562年受命入福建剿倭。在十余年中，他领军与倭寇进行大小八十余战，最后终于扫平东南沿海的倭寇之患。他所率领的军队以纪律严明、兵种齐全、装备先进、战斗力强、百战不败而著称，被称为"戚家军"。

Qi Jiguang Defeated Japanese Pirates

Qi Jiguang (1528-1587) was a famous general and military strategist in the Ming Dynasty (1368-1644). Japanese was called Wo in ancient China; therefore, the pirates from Japan were called *Wo Kou*. Qi Jiguang was born during the Jiajing Period in the mid-Ming Dynasty, when the southeastern coast was heavily harassed by Japanese pirates. They often robbed and plundered everywhere. Due to the corruption in the army of Ming Dynasty, the government troops were always defeated by Japanese pirates. In the 34th year during the reign of Jiajing (1555), Qi Jiguang was transferred to Zhejiang, where he recruited new soldiers. In 1562, he was assigned to wipe out the Japanese pirate problem in Fujian. In the next decade, he engaged in more than 80 small- and large-scale battles against the pirates, and finally put down the invasion from Japanese pirate. The army he led was marked by rigorous discipline, complete formation, advanced equipment, high combat power, and unpreventable victory. They were called "the Qi Army".

十番锣鼓

"十番锣鼓"在历史上曾有"十样锦"、"十不闲"等称谓，明代时已流行于江南一带，其中以无锡、苏州、宜兴等地最为著名。十番锣鼓的演奏者多为民间职业、半职业的艺人和道士，民间一般用于婚丧喜庆场合，或道士用来做道场及办丧事。另外，在春节、中

performed in the *Ying Hui* held on yearly basis. Its repertoire comes from folk songs as well as the opera music from the province. The organization of the band differs from place to place. The most common instruments are the pipe wind instruments, the silk string instruments and the percussion instruments. The most special among them is the percussion instruments, which display extremely complicated playing skills.

秋、赶庙会或赛龙舟时，也常见十
番锣鼓的演奏。

十番锣鼓的演奏形式有"素锣
鼓"和"荤锣鼓"两种。

"素锣鼓"又叫"清锣鼓"，
即纯粹的锣鼓乐，只用打击乐器。
其乐队组织又有粗、细之分。粗锣
鼓所使用的乐器有云锣、拍板、小
木鱼等；细锣鼓除上述乐器外还有
大小钹、中锣、春锣、风锣等。

"荤锣鼓"所演奏的是打击乐
器与管弦乐器合奏的乐曲，根据主
奏乐器和乐队组合的不同，又分为
"笛吹锣鼓"、"笙吹锣鼓"、
"粗细丝竹锣鼓"等种类。除打击

Shi Fan Luo Gu

Shi Fan Luo Gu has been called Shi Yang
Jin, Shi Bu Xian, and others in history. It
had been popular in Jiangnan (the regions
south of Yangtze River), during the
Ming Dynasty (1368-1644), especially in
Wuxi, Suzhou and Yixing. Shi Fan Luo
Gu is performed by local professionals,
semi-professional musicians or Taoists
on such occasions as weddings, funerals,
celebrations, and festivals. It is also
performed at Taoist rituals and Taoist
funeral procedures. Aside from that, it
is also performed in the Spring Festival,
Mid-Autumn Festival, temple festivals
and dragon-boat racing.

- 十番锣鼓表演（图片提供：FOTOE）
Performance of Shi Fan Luo Gu

乐器外，常用的丝竹乐器有笙、笛、箫、二胡、板胡、琵琶、三弦、月琴等。

西安鼓乐

西安鼓乐是一种主要流行于陕西省西安地区的民间吹打乐。从结构、乐谱、曲名、使用乐器等方面来看，西安鼓乐有可能源于唐代，起于宋代，兴于元明而盛于清代，经过长期的发展，特别是明清以来戏曲音乐的影响，西安鼓乐逐渐形成一套完整的大型民族古典音乐形式。

● 安塞腰鼓表演 (图片提供：CFP)
Waist Drum Performance at Ansai

Shi Fan Luo Gu is performed in two different styles: *Su Luo Gu* and *Hun Luo Gu*.

Su Luo Gu, also called *Qing Luo Gu*, refers to the pure percussion music, with only percussion instruments applied. It has two kinds of bands, thick and thin bands. Thick band employs such instruments as cloud gong, clapper and small wooden knocker; thin *Luo Gu* also contains big cymbal, small cymbal, medium gong, spring gong and wind gong besides the above list.

Hun Luo Gu performs ensembles of percussion, wind and string instruments. Based on the difference in the presiding instrument and the band formation, it can be further divided into *Di* (flute) *Chui Luo Gu*, *Sheng* (free reed mouth organ with finger holds) *Chui Luo Gu* and *Cu Xi Si Zhu* (thick or thin silk and bamboo instrument) *Luo Gu*. In addition to the percussion instrument, the commonly used instruments include *Sheng*, flute, vertical flute, *Er Hu*, *Ban Hu*, pear-shaped lute, three strings and *Yue Qin*.

Xi'an *Gu Yue*

Xi'an *Gu Yue* is a local wind and percussion music popular mainly in the

• 西安鼓乐表演（图片提供：CFP）
Performance of Xi'an *Gu Yue*

　　西安鼓乐多在每年夏秋之际，为庆贺丰收在各地举行的乡会、庙会上演奏，演奏者为各村镇组织的"鼓乐社"以及大寺院、大庙宇的鼓乐乐队。

　　西安鼓乐的演奏形式有坐乐、行乐两种。坐乐为室内演奏的鼓乐形式，有严格固定的曲式结构。所用乐器以笛为主，配以笙、管，以及各种锣、鼓、梆子等。行乐比坐乐简单，演奏以曲调为主，节奏乐器只起伴奏、击拍的作用，多用于街道行进和庙会的群众场合。西

area of Xi'an in Shaanxi Province. Based on its structure, music scores, music titles, and the instruments employed, it may originated in the Tang Dynasty (618-907), was heightened in Song Dynasty (960-1279), popularized in the Yuan Dynasty (1206-1368) and Ming Dynasty (1368-1644), and prospered in the Qing Dynasty (1644-1911). Through such a long period of development, especially through the influences of opera music in the Ming Dynasty and Qing Dynasty, Xi'an *Gu Yue* has gradually become a large-scale and complete form of classical ethnic music.

Xi'an *Gu Yue* is mostly performed in the county assembly or temple assembly in the summer and fall when good harvests are celebrated. It is performed by the *Gu Yue* clubs organized by villages or towns, or by the *Gu Yue* bands of big temples or shrines.

Xi'an *Gu Yue* is performed in the forms of sitting music or marching music. Sitting music is the indoor performance of *Gu Yue*, with strict and fixed musical structures. The employed instrument is mainly based on flute and supported by *Sheng*, oboe and various gong, drum and wooden stick. Marching music is much simpler than sitting

安鼓乐各流派保留下来的曲目与曲牌有上千首，这是一笔非常宝贵的音乐遗产。

潮州锣鼓

潮州锣鼓是流行于广东省汕头一带的一种中国传统吹打乐。它本是一种以演奏弦诗乐为主的小型吹打，后来吸收戏曲音乐发展而成。潮州锣鼓种类很多，可分为潮州大

• 潮州大鼓
Chaozhou Bass Drum

music, for the performance is based on tunes while the rhythm instruments only serve to accompany or count beats. It is performed in street marching or among the crowds in temple festivals. There are more than a thousand musical titles or *Qu Pai* preserved by each school of Xi'an *Gu Yue*. It is a valuable musical heritage.

Chaozhou *Luo Gu*

Chaozhou *Luo Gu* is a kind of Chinese traditional wind and percussion music popular in the Shantou area in Guangdong Province. It was originally a small-scale wind and percussion music based on *Xian Shi* music performance. It later absorbed opera music and is processed and developed to its current form. Chaozhou *Luo Gu* can be divided into Chaozhou big *Luo Gu*, Chaozhou small *Luo Gu* and Chaozhou *Su Luo Gu*, among which Chaozhou big *Luo Gu* is the most noted.

Chaozhou big *Luo Gu* combines big *Luo Gu* with pipe wind instruments and plucked string instruments for ensembles. The major instruments it employs are bass drum, *Da Dou* gong, big cymbal, small cymbal, big *Suo Na* trumpet and small *Suo Na* trumpet, flute, *Ye Hu*, dulcimer, *Yue Qin*, three-

鼓、潮州小锣鼓及潮州苏锣鼓等不同类别，其中最为著名的是潮州大锣鼓。

潮州大锣鼓是以大锣鼓结合吹管乐器、拉弦乐器的一种合奏形式，主要乐器有大鼓、大斗锣、大钹、小钹、大小唢呐、笛子、椰胡、扬琴、月琴、三弦、琵琶、提胡、大胡等。大锣鼓的演奏由鼓手通过鼓点、鼓的音响节奏以及手势和表情来指挥乐队，演奏时情绪饱满、变化多端，颇有气派。

潮州小锣鼓，是大锣鼓乐队中去掉了一些音响强烈而音色重浊的打击乐器，派生出来的一种合奏形式，具有轻快、明朗的特色。

潮州苏锣鼓，又名"八音"，主要流行于广东潮阳、揭阳、汕头、澄海一带。它的特点是以汉剧中的苏鼓、苏锣为主，演奏的曲目多为汉剧吹奏曲牌。

strings, pear-shaped lute, *Ti Hu* and *Da Hu*. The performance of big *Luo Gu* is conducted by the drummer through the means of drumming points, drumming rhythm, hand gestures and expressions. The performance is characterized by fully excited emotions and changeability in a stylish manner.

Chaozhou small *Luo Gu* deletes the strong-volume and heavy-tone percussion instruments from the band of big *Luo Gu* in order for the ensemble to give out a fast-paced, light and bright style.

Chaozhou *Su Luo Gu*, also known as "eight sounds" (*Ba Yin*), prevails mainly in the areas of Chaoyang, Jieyang, Shantou, and Chenghai in Guangdong Province. Its special characteristic is the featured Su drum and Su gong, which are used in Han opera. Its repertoire comes mainly from the *Qu Pai* performed in Han opera.

> 民族管弦乐队

在2000多年前的周代，中国即已形成由"八音"组成的管弦乐队。当时宫廷的雅乐便是由这种乐队来演奏的。隋唐时期的燕乐乐队，除吸收部分雅乐乐器外，还广泛采用民间、少数民族和外来的乐器，在唐代曾盛极一时。20世纪初，西洋音乐传入中国，不少音乐家和相关人士试图借鉴西洋乐队的经验，探索中国民族乐队的新形式。

作为一个多民族国家，中国有许多独特的民族乐队，如由艾捷克、热瓦普、笛子等乐器组成的维吾尔族乐队，大小芦笙组成的苗族芦笙乐队等等。而一般所说的中国民族乐队，通常是指在汉族地区流行的、主要由汉族乐器组成的管弦乐队。

> Ethnic Orchestra

Over 2,000 thousand years ago in the Zhou Dynasty (1046 B.C.-256 B.C.), an orchestra called "eight sounds" (*Ba Yin*) had already been formed. The court music *Ya* music was performed by the band of eight sounds at that time. The musical band of *Yan* music in the Sui Dynasty (581-618) and Tang Dynasty (618-907) not only incorporated some of the *Ya* music instruments, but also widely adopted those instruments from local societies, ethnic minority groups and foreign countries. Its development culminated in the Tang Dynasty. At the beginning of the 20th century, as western music was imported into China, many musicians and relevant people borrowed the experience of the western musical band for the purpose of exploring a new form of Chinese national music.

As a multi-racial country, China

• 任熏《瑶池霓裳图》（清）

Picture of Yaochi and the Flimsy Garment by Ren Xun (Qing Dynasty, 1644-1911)

has a lot of distinctive national musical bands, such as the Uygur band made up of instruments like *Aijieke*, rubab and flute, and the *Lu Sheng* musical bands of the ethnic group of Miao, which are composed of big *Lu Sheng* and small *Lu Sheng*. Generally speaking, the Chinese national musical band refers to the orchestras made up of the ethnic Han's musical instruments which prevail in the areas that the Han ethnic people inhabit.

The formation of the national orchestra has integrated the traditional silk and bamboo musical band and wind and percussion musical band, and absorbed the advantages of various instrument combinations based on the function, special characteristics and distinctive tones of each instrument. It considers such factors as the combination of the treble, mediant and bass, the balance in the volume, and the coordination in terms of the timbre, while a certain degree of imitation is made of the formation of western orchestra. Currently, the national orchestra is composed of the pipe wind instrument section, the percussion instrument section, the plucked string instrument section and the bowed string instruction section. Meanwhile, the sections of the

民族管弦乐队的编制综合了传统丝竹乐队和吹打乐队，吸取了各类乐器组合的优点，根据乐器的性能、特点和音色等情况，考虑到高、中、低声部的配合，音量的均衡与音色的协调等因素，还在部分程度上模仿了西方交响乐队的编制。现在的民族管弦乐队一般由吹管乐器组、打击乐器组、拨弦乐器组和弓弦乐器组组成，同时还为弓弦乐器组和弹弦乐器组配齐了高、中、低音声部。按规模大小，民族管弦乐队大体可分为大、中、小三种类型：

小型乐队有十人左右。主要乐器有笛子、笙、扬琴、琵琶、中阮、二胡、中胡、大胡、低胡等，多用于小型合奏和为独奏、独唱、歌舞、杂技伴奏。

中型乐队为四十人左右。主要乐器有笛、笙、唢呐、定音鼓、扬琴、柳琴、琵琶、中阮、大阮、高胡、二胡、中胡、大胡、低胡等。

大型乐队为七十人左右。是在中型乐队的基础上扩大而成，拥有高、中、低音成套唢呐。

bowed string instrument and plucked string instrument are subdivided into the treble, mediant and bass parts. According to the size, the national orchestra can be classified into three types: the large-scale orchestra, medium-scale orchestra and the small-scale orchestra.

The small-scale musical band is made up of 10 people or so. The major instruments include flute, *Sheng*, dulcimer, pear-shaped lute, medium moon-shaped lute, *Er Hu*, *Zhong Hu*, *Da Hu* and *Di Hu*. It is performed mostly in small ensembles or accompanies instrument solos, vocal solos, dances and acrobatic shows.

The medium-scale musical band is comprised of around 40 people with such major instruments as flute, *Sheng*, *Suo Na* trumpet, Timpani, dulcimer, *Liu Qin*, pear-shaped lute, medium moon-shaped lute, big moon-shaped lute, *Gao Hu*, *Er Hu*, *Zhong Hu*, *Da Hu* and *Di Hu*.

The large-scale musical band is composed of 70 people or so. The formation is expanded on the basis of the medium-scale band, with a full set of *Suo Na* trumpet in the treble, mediant, and bass parts.

● 民族管弦乐团的演出（图片提供：CFP）
Performance of the National Orchestra

民族管弦乐队的配置 Formation of the National Orchestra	
分组 Sections	乐器组成 Component Instruments
拉弦乐器组 Bowed String Instruments	二胡、中胡、革胡、倍革胡、高胡 *Er Hu, Zhong Hu, Ge Hu, Bei Ge Hu, Gao Hu*
弹拨乐器组 Plucked String Instruments	扬琴、琵琶、中阮、大阮、三弦、筝、柳琴 Dulcimer, Pear-shaped lute, Medium moon-shaped lute, Big moon-shaped lute, Three-strings, 25-stringed zither, *Liu Qin*
吹管乐器组曲笛 Pipe Wind Instruments: Flute	梆笛、新笛、唢呐（高音、中音、低音）、笙（高音、中音、低音） *Bang* flute, *Xin* flute, *Suo Na* trumpet(treble, medIant, and bass), *Sheng* (treble, mediant, and bass)
打击乐器组 Percussion Instruments	堂鼓、排鼓、碰铃、锣、云锣、吊镲、军鼓、木鱼 *Tang* drum, *Pai* drum, *Peng Ling*, Gong, Cloud gong, Suspended Cymbal, Snare drum, Wooden knocker

中国红系列

中国印
老茶具
笔墨纸砚
书法
茶马古道
古镇
古钱币
徽州艺术
紫砂壶
吉祥图案
古代兵器
古典建筑
中医
西藏艺术
佛像艺术
古铜器
梅兰竹菊
传统乐器
长城
年画
古代服饰
剪纸
中国画
中国酒
唐诗
中国节日
中国石
少数民族服饰
中国雕刻
中国扇

传统工艺品
Traditional Chinese Crafts

中国色彩
Colorful China

刺绣
Chinese Embroidery

中国禅
Zen

棋艺
Art of Chesses

宋词
Ci-Poems of the Song Dynasty

中国饮食
Chinese Food

中国名湖
Famous Lakes in China

中国料器
Chinese Glassware

帝王陵寝
Imperial Mausoleum

中华传统美德
Chinese Traditional Virtues

中国姓氏
Chinese Surnames

传统家具
Chinese Furniture

中国名山
Renowned Chinese Mountains

中国染织
Chinese Dyeing and Weaving

武术
Chinese Martial Arts

民间玩具
Folk Toys

古代教育
Education in Ancient China

中国神话传说
Chinese Mythology and Legends

古代游戏
Recreational Games in Ancient China

四大名著
Four Masterpieces of Chinese Fiction

古代科技
Ancient China's Science and Technology

金银器
Gold and Silver Wares

竹木牙角器
Art Crafts Make of Bamboo, Wood, Ivory and Horn

风筝
Kites

盆景
Bonsai

景泰蓝
Cloisonné

泥塑
Clay Sculpture

面塑
Dough Figuring

大运河
Grand Canal

历史名城
Historical Cities

中国结
Chinese Knots

兵马俑
Terracotta Army

皮影
Folk Shadow Play

中国古代帝王
Emperors of China

中国陶器
Chinese Pottery Ware

中国漆器
Chinese Lacquer Articles

中国名寺
Famous Temples in China

中国石窟
Grottoes in China

中国古桥
Ancient Bridges in China

中国古塔
Ancient Pagodas in China

中国民居
Traditional Civil Residents

民间戏曲
Traditional Folk Operas

中国灯彩
Colorful Chinese Lanterns and Lamps

诸子百家
Traditional Philosophers and Ideologists

中国牌坊
Chinese Decorated and Memorial Archways

中国茶艺
Chinese Tea Appreciation Ceremony

秦砖汉瓦
Brick of Qin Dynasty and Tile of Han Dynasty

面具
Masks

鼻烟壶
Snuff Bottles

颐和园
The Summer Palace

丝绸之路
The Silk Road

汉字
Chinese Characters

中国木偶艺术
Chinese Puppet Arts

古代兵书
Ancient Book on the Art of War

道教文化
Daoism Culture in China

古代交通
Ancient Traffic

古代壁画
Ancient Chinese Mural Painting

古代衡器
Ancient Weighing Apparatus

24节气
The Twenty-four Solar Terms

中国名泉
Famous Springs in China

长江黄河
Yangtze River and Yellow River

传统杂技
Traditional Acrobatic Arts

中国婚俗
Marriage Customs in China

匾额对联
Inscribed Tablets and Couplets

中国建筑装饰
Chinese Architectural Decoration

十二生肖
The Twelve Animals Represent Years

佩饰
Ornaments Wore by Ancient Chinese

文房清供
Stationery and Bibelot in Ancient Studies

中国祥禽瑞兽
Auspicious Beasts and Fowls in Chinese Culture